Signs of Redemption

by Christopher Karam

©2017

Cover Photography by Derek Lewis

Text copyright © 2017

All rights reserved. No part of this book may be reproduced in any manner whatsoever without written permission from the author, except in the case of brief quotations in reviews and articles.

This is a work of fiction. Names, characters, places and incidents either are the product of the author's imagination or are used fictitiously. Any resemblance to actual events, locales, organizations, or persons, living or dead, is entirely coincidental and beyond the intent of either the author or the publisher.

To Paul

Chapter I

1863

The boy was roughly nine years of age, and had just taken a sage grouse with his bow. An unusually skillful endeavor for a child, but not so for a Sioux. They were taught to hunt at a very young age and were looked upon by their parents with great pride and joy. The boy stared at the grouse. It was a celebration of life, as he thanked the bird for its sacrifice. His small hands retrieved the arrow from the bird and, after wiping the blood off with some sand, he placed it back in his quiver. The quiver was made of simple deer skin. Tanned and shaped by water and dried by the sun, it was lined with beaver fur so the arrows would not rattle. The boy's father had worked with him to make it, and the boy was proud to carry it across his back. Picking up his contribution to the family dinner, the boy walked home. He had no idea he was being watched.

Half a mile away, a buckskin-clad scout was lying belly-down on the top of a bluff, surveying the Sioux camp he had been assigned to reconnoiter. He retrieved a short, whittled-down pencil from between his teeth and scratched a few figures onto a small folded piece of paper. Collapsing his spyglass, he slowly tucked it back into the leather side-pouch on his belt and slid on his belly backwards, away from the hill's rocky peak and out of sight. Finishing his calculations, he tucked the pencil and paper back into his shirt pocket, retrieved his hat and walked back down the remainder of the steep hill to his horse.

It was the afternoon of his third day in the Black Hills, and the scout had prided himself at going undetected up to this point and he did not want that to change. The sun was starting to sink lower in the sky, and he preferred to make camp a bit farther away from the Sioux. Tomorrow, he would head back to the battalion, which was several miles from the Sioux camp. There, he would write his report and submit it to the colonel in charge. The report would confirm the Sioux camp was still active and would detail the strength of their numbers. His calculations would identify how many miles away the camp was from their battalion, how many horses they had, the configuration of the camp and even include the prevailing wind direction.

Two days after the scout reported in, the battalion rode off to battle. Since his primary work was done, the scout was instructed to hold back and later ride out with the group of soldiers that would round up horses in the aftermath of the confrontation.

Entering the valley from the south, the first two companies rode at a slow gallop. As hundreds of men entered the meadow within a mile of the Lakota lodges, cries went up from posted Sioux sentries, but they were too late to make a difference. The cavalry rode through the valley with a thunderous noise. Soldiers fired at the warriors who were appearing from their teepees, armed with lances or bows. Some warriors grabbed lances that were resting against the outside of their lodges in an attempt to spear or knock riders from their mounts. Without enough time to get to their own horses, the warriors tried as best they could to fight back, but the superior numbers of mounted cavalry extinguished any attempt of a counterattack with bullet and cutlass. Very few cavalry soldiers fell from the saddle as they rode among the teepees firing on the Indians. Women who dared pick up a bow or lance, were also quickly shot down or trampled under the hooves of the cavalry horses.

Coming upon the bloodshed, the group assigned to capture the horses rode into the valley, and the scout's eyes were opened to some of the darker horrors of war. With a victory looking to be well within hand, the colonel had suddenly given orders to burn the teepees. This didn't make sense! "Why?!" he screamed aloud.

The scout heard women and children screaming from being trapped within their simple buffalo skin structures as soldiers began taking sticks from the surrounding campfires and prepared to set the teepees afire.

He felt sick and angry at the same time, stunned by what he was seeing. This was not the organized battle he envisioned. Planned tactics were being replaced with chaos. He had seen enough. The scout abandoned his group and rode headlong toward a soldier who held a torch near one of the teepees. As the scout closed in on the soldier, he leapt from his horse, throwing the soldier from his own mount. They hit the ground hard. Hearing a child's screams and cries from within the teepee, the scout knocked the torch from the soldier's hand, which fell at the base of the lodging. As the soldier went for his pistol, the scout struck him a heavy blow on the chin with his fist, knocking him down. Another cavalry officer, seeing the confrontation between the cavalry man and the scout, rode up and struck the scout across the back of the head with the butt of his saber. The scout fell forward onto the buffalo skin teepee and rolled to the ground as the teepee caught fire.

Minutes went by before the scout regained his senses, woken by the heat from the burning hide. Standing, but still dizzy, he moved to the back of the teepee and cut it open with his knife. He then motioned for the mother to bring her child and to come with him. At first the Sioux mother refused and screamed something at the scout. Even though he knew several Lakota words from local traders; this he did not understand.

The scout continued to motion to the woman to leave the teepee, saying "hee," which meant "come." The woman realized this man whose clothes were different from the uniforms of the soldiers who were attacking her village, was her only hope for safety. She decided the scout would have to be trusted, and followed him while clutching her small child close to her breast.

Grabbing the reins of his horse, the scout leapt into the saddle. The mother handed her child to the scout, as she swung a leg up and onto the back of the horse. Seated behind him, he passed the child back to her and the three rode off toward the opposite corner of the valley, away from the fighting.

As the warm sun shone down on the young Sioux child clinging to his mother, he had no idea of the suffering and injustice that was being inflicted on his people; nor would he understand the fulfillment towards the claim of manifest destiny for one civilization and the eventual termination of a unique and proud way of life for another.

In the distance, the firing of rifles mingled with the war cries of braves as they fought desperately to defend their camp. Screams from the women and children continued throughout the attack. Satisfied with the burning lodges, the colonel considered his objective achieved and gave the order to pull back and regroup. The main companies rode out of the valley toward the northeast. Those who had been assigned to raid the horses in the meadow began to round them up.

The few remaining braves, too small in number to mount a counter-attack on the cavalry, spent their frustrations on those left in the field who had been killed by lance or bow. Screams of mourning came from the few remaining women, kneeling beside their burning lodges.

The scout slowed his horse a mile from the battle after crossing the river at a low point. Smoke clouds from the burning lodges were still in view, as he delivered mother and child to the ground within the confines of the riverbed. Hearing a thundering of hooves getting closer, he turned toward the northern end of the valley. As he peered over the top of the riverbed, he saw what looked to be roughly thirty Sioux riders racing southward into the valley toward their burning village. Perhaps these warriors had been part of a raiding party. Upon reaching the camp, the warriors quickly surrounded and killed the soldiers who had remained to raid the horses. The irony hung heavy as the scout realized that in saving the lives of the woman and child, he most certainly had saved his own as well.

The scout then turned his attention back to the woman holding her child. Stunned at what he had witnessed, the only thing he could think to do was place his hand on his heart and say, "chahn-day shee-chay."

which he knew meant "I'm sorry" in Lakota. With that, he rode out the opposite end of the valley, never looking back.

Chapter II

1904

The steam from the 10:05 "20th Century Limited" covered the boardwalk in a cloudy mist. It was still pretty cold for late April, and the people of New York had yet to give up their heavy winter coats. Passengers waiting in line shuffled directly behind each other with little to no gaps in between as they boarded the long black train. Each one anticipated the step up into the entryway of the passenger car, which was a welcome break from the brisk morning wind.

James Riley had been working during the winter months, guiding various hunters in search of deer and bear. The winter was a long one, and at the age of sixty-two, his body had grown tired of the long treks into the woods. He often contemplated retirement, yet each fall brought back the familiar feeling of adventure that made his soul sing. The guide business wouldn't make you rich, but it placed James in an environment he loved dearly, and for the last thirty-nine years he had called the Adirondacks his home. He had been married for the past fourteen years to Wendy Thompson, whom he had met five years after her husband was killed in a logging accident.

He had enjoyed watching his stepson Andrew grow up in Altamont, and the two had grown close. But at the age of twenty-one, Andrew had traveled out west to Montana and stayed there after marrying a fine Shoshone Indian girl named Willow. Two years later, Andrew and

Willow proudly wrote to James and Wendy about their newly born son, whom they named Lewis. Wendy had traveled west two weeks earlier and was already staying with Andrew, Willow and the baby. James was eager to meet his grandson and, after staying behind to finish the work he had lined up for the season, he could now look forward to a long rest and spending time with his family.

He always preferred to travel light, and stowed his one bag above the seat before sitting down by the window. The bag contained just what he felt was necessary for the trip and nothing more, a habit he had learned from his time as a scout in the U.S. Army. In addition to his clothes and shaving kit, he had packed his .32-20 Colt. At first he had thought about leaving it behind, but reconsidered, as he knew Montana was still a rugged country. As the passenger car started to fill up, a tall lean man, close to his own build, walked past him and took a seat on the opposite side of the car. He wore a tan slicker with a wool jacket underneath. His hair was dark gray in color with his mustache and beard a slightly lighter shade. The man opened a newspaper and began to read.

There was a curiosity about this man that puzzled James. The more he looked at the man, the more he felt he knew him.

Thinking of whom he had met recently, he eventually decided that he knew the man from his past. In fact, he was certain. He studied his eyes and used the cover of the man's newspaper to try and picture him without his beard, looking away every so often to not get caught staring. The more he studied the man, the more his gut gave him an uncomfortable feeling, but he wasn't sure why. He had met many men

during the past thirty-plus years of guiding people into the Adirondack wilderness and most he could remember if placed to the task. But he realized that Father Time can do quite a bit of change to a man's appearance, just like himself.
The conductor gave his last shout of "All aboard!" as the train started down the westward rails. James opened the railway map, which he'd highlighted in pencil all the stops he'd make on his way to Chicago before changing trains and continuing west to Montana.

It was about thirty minutes into the trip that James figured he just might go up to the man and introduce himself, but something inside kept him feeling cautious. He listened intently to see if anyone seated next to the man spoke to him or called out his name, but the man appeared to be traveling alone and kept to himself.

It was another forty minutes or so when the man became slightly uncomfortable in his chair and pushed his leg partly into the isle to stretch, catching James' attention. At first, the motion made James stretch himself. Almost the way one yawn will cause another person to yawn themselves. It was then that James saw something he hadn't noticed before. The man's boots were black and looked to be Army issue. More specifically, cavalry boots. James searched his thoughts back to when he had served. It had been more than thirty-five years since he had been a scout for the Army out west. Could he have served with this man?

Growing frustrated with not being able to place the face, James decided to focus his thoughts on his new grandson in Montana. It would be a five-day trip by train and while he appreciated the speed of the iron horse, he felt slightly envious of his own younger self, who would have made the journey by a real horse, camping under the stars and taking in the smells and sights of the hills, mountains and prairies. He laughed to himself at the thought of his sixty-two-year-old body enduring thunderstorms, flooded creek beds, long days in the saddle and hunting for his own food. It had been a while since he had skinned a rattler or was quick enough to shoot a jack rabbit. Suddenly, the train didn't seem like such a bad idea after all.

It was ten o'clock on the second day when the train made its stop in Chicago, Illinois. He had a little over an hour to kill and contemplated walking around the city for a bit, or maybe getting himself a steak before boarding the train to take him further west. He had never been to Chicago and had heard a few of his clientele speak of the large city where all the beef came in by rail. He sat on a bench for a while, watching all the people walk past. He found it interesting to see the modern clothing of the day and wondered where they all were headed. Before changing trains, James decided to first use the bathroom in the station.

Entering the washroom in the station, he placed his hat down on the rim of the sink next to him. Looking in the mirror, he saw the man with the cavalry boots walk into the bathroom stall behind him and close the door. James opened the hot water spigot on the sink and waited until it ran warm, and then splashed his face thoroughly several times. The warm water felt good as it ran over his face and down his cheeks. As he looked up to view his face in the mirror above the sink, he could see the man exit the stall and walk toward him and stop a few feet behind him. A deep voice called out, "James Riley?"

"Yes," James answered as he spun around, his face still wet. "My name is Captain Forsythe. I'm placing you under arrest for desertion."

James' mind went blank. He felt a cold chill go up his back. "You... you must be joking," James stammered!

"Afraid not," said the man calmly, as he handed James a piece of paper which bore his name and listed the circumstances for his arrest. James read the paper and for a moment looked past it. He noticed the man's other hand rested on the ivory grips of his revolver, which was still holstered, but unlashed.

"I've been searching for you on and off for quite some time, 'Private' Riley. I almost gave up looking for you until I happened to come across a man who spoke highly of an Adirondack guide named James Riley. I had talked to quite a few people in the area who knew you as James Kelly. You should have kept the alias."

James answered with a mix of anger and sarcasm. "I figured enough time went by where the Army really wouldn't care to send a bounty hunter after an old worn-out scout," said James.

"I prefer Recovery Agent, Private, and to be exact, the Army doesn't really care as much as I do. I happen to make my living this way and you never really escaped my mind completely; that is since we served in the same company."

"You served under Lieutenant Newport?"

"No, not Newport. Under Colonel Reynolds out of Fort Fedderman. You still don't remember me, do you? No matter. Bottom line is you abandoned your company. Enough talk Private Riley; put these on." Captain Forsythe handed James a pair of shackles for his wrists, and James glanced at Forsythe's right hand. It was still on his ivory-handled Colt, so he put them on as asked.

"Let's go," said Forsythe as he motioned towards the door.
As James was escorted back to the boardwalk, he became curious as to why Forsythe walked him past the waiting train.
"Aren't we going to board?" asked James.
"We'll be heading west, Private."
"I was heading west, to Montana. Where are you taking me?"
"We're boarding another train."
"My family is waiting for me in Montana. Please, can't we make another arrangement here? I promise I'll come back after I see my grandson."

"No deal," said Forsythe.
He walked James past a group of people who stared at them, and then sat him down on a bench. For twenty minutes they waited in silence, watching those who stared walk back and forth. James searched his mind for any scrap of memory, which might lead him to remember this man, but none came to him.

Then, a five-car train could be seen coming around the bend north of them. It slowed as it approached the station and let its steam purge from the large boiler.

"Here, this is our train," said Captain Forsythe. "Move, lest I have to assist you." He prodded James lightly with his finger, and the two boarded the train.

Chapter III

The Sioux warrior sat in front of the low-burning fire, his long gray hair draped over the front of his stern-looking face as he cupped the billowing smoke with his hands and washed it over his chest, face and hair. Ogaleesha was considered very old for a brave. Many of the other warriors he'd grown up with had been killed during the years of the Plains Indian Wars.

Ogaleesha, whose name means "Wears a Red Shirt," spent what was supposed to be the best years of his life fighting his way through many battles and watching his people slowly disappear. His name was given to him after he had been shot in the chest by an Army rifle when he was only nineteen. His buckskin shirt had soaked up the blood from his wound, but even wounded he had fought on, killing the soldier who shot him. When he was in his twenties, Ogaleesha fought under Crazy Horse, whom he admired for his strength and well-planned strategies. He had fought ferociously at the Fetterman Massacre, where his crimson attire would darken further, only this time with the blood of his enemies.

He savored the victory at the battle of Little Big Horn, where the Oglala and Lakota tribes of the Sioux, joined by the Cheyenne and Arapaho, defeated the U.S. Seventh Cavalry, and later helped drive back the white man's army at the battle of Tongue River.

Ogaleesha continued to be loyal to Crazy Horse, even when many other followers abandoned him after food supplies dwindled over a very long and harsh winter. But eventually, Ogaleesha knew Crazy Horse could not continue to evade the growing U. S. Army for much longer. With his people suffering from starvation and their ammunition sources depleted, Crazy Horse led over a thousand of his remaining followers to a reservation near Fort Robinson and surrendered. Ogaleesha wanted to fight on, but Crazy Horse understood it was best for the remainder of his people to live the rest of their lives in peace, even if it was to be on a reservation. And it was on the reservation, where Ogaleesha had started to learn to read the English language and gradually adapt to the new way of life.

Many months later, the day came when Ogaleesha heard the news of Crazy Horse's death. Rumor had passed down that he had left the reservation to care for his sick wife. When challenged with a demand to return to the reservation, he refused and was stabbed by a soldier's bayonet while resisting arrest. This infuriated Ogaleesha to the point that he wanted to abandon any thought of living quietly on a reservation, but his younger brother Mato convincingly talked to him about carrying on with their life as it was.

Not long after, the Sioux were moved to the Pine Ridge Reservation located at the southern end of the Badlands in South Dakota. Only a small percentage of the thirty-four hundred square miles was suitable for agriculture. Over ten thousand Sioux men, women and children were to share and live off this land.

It was five years after the death of Crazy Horse that Ogaleesha took a wife named Tashina, which means "Walks With Her Shawl" in English. Two years later, they gave birth to a son, Chaska, appropriately meaning "First Son."

Farming was poor on the Pine Ridge reservation land. The Sioux had originally been settled under wetter than normal seasons, and subsequent years led to drought. The soil was ideal for short prairie grass, but there wasn't enough water available to irrigate large crops of corn. Many like Ogaleesha, decided hunting and fishing must remain an integral part of their lives.

Some of the braves that lived nearby, still spoke of the Ghost Dances and believed the spirits of their dead ancestors would fight on their behalf to make the white men leave, and bring peace, prosperity, and unity to Indian peoples throughout the region.

Ogaleesha did not believe in such religion, as he only believed what he could see and experience for himself. To him, it was a waste of time to dance and sing for victory. Only fighting for victory would drive out the white men, and those ways were lost to him now.

When Ogaleesha and Tashina's son turned ten years old, they decided a great gift was in order so that Chaska could hunt at the side of his father for years to come. Ogaleesha decided to make a bow for his son, using the old ways of his fathers. He worked hard to find and carve the right piece of cedar to make the shaft. He then soaked the shaft in a shallow stream for two days. He needed sinew for the string, and decided to hunt a mule deer on the reservation and use its leg sinews for the bowstring. The meat would then feed his family and his friends when they celebrated Chaska's tenth year.

It took three days of tracking a herd of mule deer over the hilly terrain of grasses and rocks, before he was able to make the killing shot with his rifle. It was a fine male deer, weighing roughly one hundred and thirty-five pounds. He made a travois and lashed it to his horse so he could drag the deer behind as he rode.

On his trek home, Ogaleesha felt strange. A feeling of hopelessness came over him. It seemed out of place, considering his recent achievement. But he put great value in the visions and emotions Crazy Horse had shared with his people. If this meant something, he wanted to be back home with his wife and child. He doubled his pace as he made his way back to familiar land and eventually, the family teepee. The sun had just inched below the horizon and Ogaleesha became nervous and excited at the same time as he anticipated sharing the news of his hunt with his wife. As he opened the flap to the teepee, he noticed no burning coals in the center fire ring. No sign of his wife or son. "Where could they be? Were they with Mato's family?

Ogaleesha, leaving the deer behind, ran as fast as his legs would carry him over the mile distance to Mato's teepee. He yelled his brother's name as he approached. Mato emerged from his teepee with his arms open. "Brother, come here," he said. "We must talk."

It was then that Mato tried his best to console his brother.

He explained how Tashina had taken Chaska to the Ghost Dance ceremony at Wounded Knee Creek, despite Mato asking her not to go. It was a ceremony to give hope to their people, but the U.S. Government saw it as an uprising and quickly sent troops to stop the Ghost Dance. When a sole brave refused to give up his rifle to the soldiers, the shooting broke out. Hundreds of U.S. troops opened fire on all Sioux involved in the ceremony. When it was over, one hundred and fifty men, women and children were dead, with another fifty wounded. With much grief, Mato explained to his brother how his wife and son had fatally fallen as victims in the tragedy.

Ogaleesha fell to his knees and screamed at the top of his lungs. When his brother tried to console him, he gripped Mato around the waist with a bear hug and struck his brother's back with his clenched fists, then slowly released him, as he sank to his knees and pounded the dry earth. He cried a Sioux warrior's song of death.

Over the next few days, Ogaleesha avoided contact, distancing himself from others. For six days Mato could not find him. On the seventh day, Ogaleesha returned to Mato and asked him to find the other surviving braves from Crazy Horse's tribe, and to call a meeting that evening in Mato's teepee. The old warrior arrived at the teepee wearing a buckskin shirt, which was dyed with the blood of the deer he had killed. He sat cross-legged in front of the slow burning fire. Twelve old warrior faces glowed in the firelight around the large circle. Not one of them had seen less than forty-eight winters. Ogaleesha had seen more than fifty.

"The time has come to leave this place of death," Ogaleesha stated to the group. He knew some of them had lost family members as well in the great massacre.

"Who will join me?" Ogaleesha asked.

Seven of the Twelve, including Mato, raised their hands in accord. "Gather your horses, your guns and other belongings. We will leave tomorrow morning and head west," he said in a somber tone.

The small group of eight fled the reservation, swearing never to return. Under Ogaleesha's command, the band of eight warriors rode to the southwest, traveling between Colorado and New Mexico where they could hide in the rough country from their pursuers and live as bandits, robbing from the white men who had pushed them from their birth place. When they would rustle only a few cattle from white men's ranches for food, it went unnoticed. When they hid out in the hills and smoked the beef so it lasted for weeks, they kept their fires low. The ranchers were none the wiser because they often accounted for a lost cow here and there due to predators or harsh weather. The ranchers were only concerned with thieves who stole large groups of their cattle.

Ogaleesha's band of braves also robbed from those who traveled in small groups, such as prospectors or farmers. He would often send out two or three braves at different times, so his entire band was rarely together at one specific time or place. Ogaleesha was not a greedy man, and the braves that rode with him held him in high regard for his tactical prowess and strong leadership. They attacked in remote locations, which kept any news of their numbers or whereabouts almost non-existent. Most of their victims ended up as a meal for scavenging coyotes or the buzzards.

Sometimes, Ogaleesha's band would round up wild horses or a few of the rancher's cattle and trade them to Mexican bandits at small shanty-type outposts just over the border. These Mexicans were continually evading the Guardia Rural, which was Mexico's version of mounted police. Ogaleesha would trade horses to the bandits for ammunition, food, extra clothing and U. S. newspapers, which he would read whenever he could to expand his knowledge of the English language, as well as to see if his band's activities were mentioned in the papers of the white man. It was as if Ogaleesha was fighting his very own small, well-organized war.

For several years, the band of eight existed in the most remote stretches of the southwest, stealing from and killing those unfortunate enough to cross their path.

Still, the old warrior sat in front of the low-burning fire, his long gray hair draped over the front of his face, and he cupped the billowing smoke with his hands and washed it over his chest, face and hair. He turned his head slowly as he heard someone walking up behind him. It was Mato.

"What news do you bring me, brother?"

Mato dropped a tattered newspaper in front of Ogaleesha, who picked it up and glanced through its pages.

"So, it is true. The white men are pulling the gold from the San Juan Mountains. They carry it out in small shipments using the iron horse."
"What do they do with this gold?" asked Mato.

"It is what they use in trade, and it is the most valuable of things to the white men. They kill each other over it. Even the Mexicans treasure the yellow rocks. We could use these rocks to rebuild our nation again, south of the great river."

"How would we do this?" asked Mato.

"We will find a way to take it from them, and then sell it to the greedy Mexicans for land, horses and cattle. We will then go back to the reservation and take ourselves new Sioux brides and free them from the land of death. We will make the Sioux nation strong again."

Again, Mato asked, "How will we do this?"

"Carefully, like the coyote," Ogaleesha answers. "Yet bold, like the puma. You should trust me, my brother. I have a plan."

Chapter IV

Manuel and José Garcia waited in the dark cantina with a half-empty bottle of mescal, listening to the man in the corner with the partially torn sombrero, play the guitar. The brothers had often used the cantina as a place of business, and tonight was no different. They were to meet the two Indians who were bringing in another fine herd of mustangs. Tonight, promised to be the largest group yet.

Their two Sioux contacts gladly accepted food and ammunition in trade for mustang horses, which the Garcia brothers, in turn, sold to independent ranchers who opposed Presidente Porfirio Díaz, at a healthy price of course. Manuel prided himself on the money he made over the past several months. The two Sioux Indians never spoke about names or places, or tried to bargain a better trade value for the horses. They simply would provide a list of what they required and then days later would meet the Garcia brothers at the cantina. The four men would then ride out to a location where the horses were held in a makeshift corral. Each time the location was different. They would exchange the goods as payment, and then the Sioux would ride away to the north, and back across the border.

Manuel poured what remained in his shot glass down his throat and looked over at his brother as he thumped the glass down on the shoddy, unleveled table with enough force that it wiggled slightly, almost tipping the remainder of the bottle. José's hand quickly darted out and steadied the bottle before it fell.

"What is wrong with you brother? We still have business to attend to. You can always come back to get drunk later."

Manuel's speech was slurred by the strength of the mescal. His spurs jingled as he swung his legs up on the table and leaned back in his chair.

"José... tonight we celebrate buying the largest herd of mustangs so far this year. We always get the better of those primitivos. But we don't mind, do we?"

José laughed in confidence, deciding to join his brother in another shot and filled his glass from the half-empty bottle. Throwing back the smoky liquid, he wiped off the mescal that had run down his chin with his sleeve, and then pulled his revolver from its holster to check the cartridges in the cylinder. He had a habit of checking what he had already checked an hour earlier.

"Did you also bring the la dinamita?"

"Sí, hermano. Twelve sticks with caps and fuses as agreed. I rolled them up in my saddle blanket. The remainder of their goods is on the pack mule. I wonder what those primitivos will do with it?"

"They'll probably use it on the gringos. They still hate them more than the Pawnee."

Manuel laughed, but then stopped and turned his head toward the cantina door as the sound of two approaching riders grew louder and louder and then stopped. Manuel and José stood up from their stools and walked outside on the front porch, their hands always close to their sidearms.

"Buenas noches, amigos," said Manuel with a wide smile.

Manuel called many of his business associates friends, but that was just for appearances. He really didn't trust any of them farther than he could throw them.

"How many?"

"Twenty-one," answered the Sioux with the red shirt.

José grew slightly nervous as this number was not what he and his brother had agreed to. The other very large Indian leaned back on his horse, never taking his eyes off José's right hand, which was close to his sidearm.

"Amigo, I thought we had agreed on twenty-eight ponies. La dinamita is very hard to come by these days," said Manuel.

"It is all we could round up this time. They are fine, spirited ponies. You will have no trouble selling them. We ride now."

With that, the two Sioux turned their horses and rode off into the sage brush. They led the Mexican brothers for a few miles over arroyos and up into the rocks until they came to a steep walled canyon. With the path narrowing and the walls gradually growing higher the further into the canyon they traveled, the riders rode single file. Manuel could not see Ogaleesha, who led the way, as his vision was almost completely blocked by Mato, who rode directly in front of Manuel.

Mato was extremely large for a Sioux warrior. His frame almost made the horse he rode look slightly small, even though it stood fourteen hands high. There were many small rocks on the ground and every so often one of the horses would misstep slightly, sending a few rocks rolling back down the path.

After a short time, the riders came to a makeshift gate where the path widened a bit. The gate was constructed of two long pieces of cedar about chest high, bound together with rawhide. It was positioned across two large stacks of rocks, with each stack forming a cradle at the top to hold the cedar logs firmly in place. Mato dismounted and lifted both of the logs, which looked to easily weigh over two hundred pounds. He then walked it backwards and placed it on the ground with a deep thump. The group moved forward over the logs single file, with Ogaleesha ordering Mato to stay behind at the gate. Mato simply nodded his head and turned his mount to face down the path from which they came. He pulled his old rifle from his scabbard and cradled it across his forearm.

Ogaleesha proceeded to lead the Mexicans further up the pass. The walls of the canyon were now a full fifteen feet or more above their heads. José did not like the confined space, but it was too late to turn back now. He followed Manuel's horse, hoping for the canyon to open up somewhere ahead. Suddenly, Ogaleesha stopped and listened. The Mexicans saw how still Ogaleesha was, so they listened too. Manuel could hear nothing but his horse breathing.

"Stay here while I ride ahead," Ogaleesha said to the two men. "My braves have been instructed to protect our herd, so I must show myself first. With that, Ogaleesha trotted up the path, waving his hand back and forth above his head.

"I do not like this place so much," José whispered to Manuel. "It's too confining."
"Here. Take a swig of this. It will help your nerves." Manuel tossed a half empty bottle of Mescal to José.

Manuel himself also felt a bit nervous, but he didn't want to tell José that. He tried to calm his thoughts by focusing on the money they would make after they profited from the ponies. After all, other than a different location, it was the same as the other times they had traded goods for horses from the Sioux. Each time, Ogaleesha would ride ahead to alert his braves of their presence. Soon, they would have more money than they had seen in years.

José uncorked the bottle and the slight echo could be heard bouncing off the canyon walls. He giggled to himself at the noise and then tilted his head back to take a large swig. He looked up at the bubbles in the bottle, as the mescal flowed into his mouth. Just then a small pebble hit the bottle which made a light "ping" as it bounced off the glass. With his head still tilted back, he looked up past the bottle and saw movement from above. Suddenly, his eyes grew wide and he choked mid-swallow, as tons of boulders rained down on him from both sides of the canyon walls above.

The glass bottle shattered and his horse neighed as it reared, throwing José from the saddle. When José tried to stand to remount his horse, a large rock hit his head and knocked him to the ground. In a panic, Manuel took the reins of his horse in one hand and held his other arm above his head to protect himself as best he could. When he tried to spin his horse around to head back down the path, the steed was knocked to the ground by the many rocks falling from above. Ogaleesha waited until the dust cleared from the narrow corridor, then ordered two of his braves down the path. In each of their hands they held a lever action rifle. As they slowly walked down the path, the echo of a chambered round could be heard.

Chapter V

James rested his head against the window of the train, taking in the scenery of the San Juan Mountains in the distance. They had traveled further southwest than he had anticipated, and had switched off lines a few times over the past two days. When they reached Cheyenne, Wyoming, they stopped briefly at a station. Several passengers got off the train before it started heading further south on a less traveled line. The route became even more complex as it changed tracks twice more, heading further southwest all the time until it came to a small mining town. The railway appeared to go no further south from this point, but rather looked to loop back around to the north. James could see a few riders dressed in army uniforms ride up to the train in a small wagon pulled by two draft horses, with one of the men holding a rifle across his lap. He was curious as to what was in the wagon, but then lost sight of them as they moved farther down the train and out of his view.

A few minutes later, the train started up again around a large loop and eased back up into the mountains over a series of small wooden trestles. Curious still why the train should travel out this far off the main line for such a quick stop, he raised an eyebrow and turned toward Captain Forsythe.
The captain looked over at him. "Mail delivery," he said, and went back to reading his paper.

It certainly was a beautiful remote country, James thought to himself as the train headed back to the northeast. He had wished his time with the army would have given him the chance to enjoy what was here.

As the train came around a bend in the tracks, it approached the timber bridge over the Winding Gulch riverbed. Normally, the river below would be rushing with water this time of year, but the recent drought left it with not even a trickle. The half-mile-long span was built from hundreds of round wood pole sections, with each section being roughly fifteen feet apart. Each section was reinforced with a diagonal "X" brace. From a mile away, the whole thing looked like a giant spider web of straight and angled lines.

Suddenly, there was a loud explosion a hundred yards in front of the train. The vibration could be felt through all of the cars. As the rear passenger car cleared the tall pines and came around the bend, onlookers could see from their windows, pieces of wood debris catapulting into the air followed by an ominous dark gray cloud. The explosion had created a twenty-foot gap in the bridge, just ahead of the engine. Where straight steel rails had lay just seconds earlier, there was now a twisted mass of metal and shattered ties. Bridge bracings, closest to the rails were shattered. In other areas, some of the bracings which looked to still be intact, were displaying long and deep cracks. The engineer immediately pulled the brake for the locomotive and tender car. The brakes screeched with a terrible high pitch as the steel wheels strained to hold the giant leviathan on the tracks. Long streams of metal sparks flew into the air creating a pyrotechnic wonder, which some might call beautiful if it were not for what was to follow.

With such a short distance to cover, the brakes could not stop the powerful train in time. The already cracked beams closest to the gap gave way under the tremendous weight. The locomotive engine went over the edge first, followed immediately by the tender car and the first passenger car. Occupants screamed in terror as their car suddenly tipped forward. There was nowhere to go inside the tightly packed train. Some passengers threw their arms out and gripped the bench seats in front of them. Others reached up and clasped the luggage racks above their heads in hopes of steadying themselves. None of this mattered in the least. Passenger's personal bags flew off of their overhead compartments. The porter's tea trolley careened forward, smashing into the front of the car, shattering cups and saucers. One tall man who stood up in the rear of the car flipped head first into the seat in front of him, his feet flailing in the air.

Like links in a chain, one after another, the cars were pulled over the edge and plummeted down the mountainside over a hundred and fifty feet to the riverbed below. The mighty engine crashed nose first into the ground, with the large boiler exploding on impact. Hundreds of pieces of hot sheet iron and bolts from the boiler shot skyward as a black cloud billowed up from the ground. Immediately, the tender car landed on top of the engine, ejecting its load of coal over the surrounding area, with the first passenger car following. It landed vertically on top of the engine and tender car with a great crash. The force of the landing broke the cast iron and wooden benches from their anchors. Bones cracked as bodies flew forward, slamming one on top of another like sardines cramped into a can. The screaming was then drowned out with what sounded like crashes of thunder, as the giant metal and wood forms smashed and twisted into a terrible pile.

As the second passenger car shot forward, leaving the twisted steel tracks, it spun sideways and broke away from the forward car, careening off the side of the wooden trestle with tremendous force before it, too, spun and fell to the riverbank below with a great crash, adding to the pile of debris. This caused the third passenger car in line to also pitch and roll. But since this car had not yet reached the gap in the tracks, it teetered and rolled off onto the steep embankment, taking the next car containing the army's horses with it, which broke free from the caboose. With a hail of whinnies and neighs, the car with the horses tore away from the third passenger car, digging its front end into the earth, then tipping head over heels onto its roof. It slid down the hill like a giant toboggan, slamming into pine trees and cracking them off at their bases, before rolling down the remainder of the steep embankment.

The third passenger car then spun and crashed into one of the bridge pilings, rolling the remainder of the way down the embankment before coming to rest in a cloud of dust. Only the lone caboose car came to a halt just shy of heading into the abyss, its brakes holding fast at the last possible moment. Three stunned men exited the caboose and walked over to view the wreckage below. One started to cautiously make his way along the edge of the trestle to see if there were any survivors below. He'd made it almost a third of the way down when a gunshot echoed across the gulch; the man dropped onto the dirt and his lifeless body rolled a short way before coming to rest upon one of the trestle pilings. Several more shots rang out, and the other two men from the caboose also lay dead. Out from the tree line, rode Ogaleesha with the seven other braves behind him.

The last brave in line was leading two ponies. Each pony had a man draped over the saddle with his wrists and ankles bound under the pony's belly. The men's lifeless bodies bounced around as the ponies trotted along. The line of warriors stopped when they arrived at the chasm created by the explosion. The grim leader watched as the other braves gathered brush and set the caboose on fire. They yelled and waved their rifles above their heads as they watched it burn.

At the bottom of the gulch, the pile of wrecked cars burned hot, fueled by the coal which was strewn all over the wreckage. The Indians rode down to look inside the car with the horses. A soldier was still alive inside, but pinned down by one of the horses. As the braves approached the car, the soldier leaned and stretched for his rifle, but it was out of reach. The braves fired their rifles into the car and the soldier moaned and then lay still. One of the braves dismounted and pulled a large steel box from the wrecked car. Another helped him drag it several yards away and then they both fired at the padlock, which held the box shut. They then smashed it with their rifle butts several times and the lock broke open. Taking several sacks from the box, they tied them around their saddle blankets.

Approaching the third passenger car with caution, they looked in through the smashed windows and saw that the passengers were all piled toward one end. None of them appeared to be moving. Ogaleesha instructed a couple of braves to cut the ropes that bound the two dead bodies to the ponies. The braves then pushed the dead men off their mounts and onto the ground, arranging the bodies as if they had been shot in a skirmish with the soldiers' car. They next stuffed brush into one of the windows and set the car ablaze before riding off to the south.

Inside the third passenger car, James Riley stirred. A sharp pain emanated from his left shoulder as he tried to move. There was a man on top of his back and a woman across his legs pinning him down. James shook his head as he tried to regain his senses. He craned his neck around enough to see that the coach car was on its roof. He heard a moan from a short distance away, but couldn't tell who it was coming from. He smelled smoke and heard the lapping of flames, and then the cracking and hissing of wood as it burned. His hands were still cuffed together. Pulling his arms free from under the man, he was able to maneuver himself out from under the bodies.

Sitting up, he looked at his left shoulder, which had a piece of glass embedded in it. It must have come from one of the windows. In spite of the handcuffs, James was able to reach high enough to pull the glass shard out of his arm. As he threw it aside, blood started to flow down his arm from the open wound. He couldn't wrap his handkerchief around the wound with his hands cuffed, so he tore off a piece of his shirt sleeve with his teeth. He screamed as he stuffed the material into his wound. It took a few moments for him to gather himself, taking slow, deep breaths to keep from passing out.

He examined the body of the man, which now was to the side of him. He was clearly dead, as his neck had been partially severed by a large piece of glass. The young woman beside him stared into emptiness, unblinking. James reached over to her and softly closed her eyes. "Her dress seemed so pretty," he thought to himself. She must have been on her way to visit someone. The flames were now engulfing the end of the coach and brought his thoughts back to the situation at hand. He tried not to panic, but knew he had to get out quickly. As he started to crawl toward the far door away from the fire, he came across the captain, who was pinned down by the body of an elderly woman. Forsythe stirred and appeared to be semi-conscious as he moaned something about his arm. James tried to pull him free, but needed better leverage. Bodies, even small women, were very heavy when they lay as dead weight.

He checked the elderly woman for a pulse and felt none. Her neck flopped loosely as he tried to turn her over. Realizing she was dead, he pushed the body aside with his legs until she rolled off of Forsythe. James then positioned himself behind the captain and used his bound hands to pull him by the back of his coat collar, sliding him over bodies as they made their way toward the door. When they reached the opening, James pulled him several yards away from the coach car.

Forsythe gasped to fill his lungs with the clean air outside the coach and then seemed to pass out in pain. James stumbled back to check for any other survivors. Crawling inside the passenger car, James spotted his bag off to the side. He managed to opened it and found his Colt revolver. He no sooner tucked the .32-20 into his belt, when he heard a soft moan.

By now, the coach was almost completely filled with smoke. James scanned through the gray clouds for any sign of movement. He spotted a middle-aged black woman reaching for one of the metal bench frames above her. She, too, was pinned down by two bodies. James ripped part of the shirt off a dead man's back and loosely stuffed it in his own mouth to filter some of the smoke.

When he reached the woman, she mumbled something quietly to him, which he could not understand. There was no time for conversation, anyhow. He quickly grabbed the woman by one of her arms and pulled with all the strength he had left to free her. She kicked and pushed with her feet until they finally succeeded in freeing her. The two then crawled out of the coach, coughing and gagging to push the thick smoke from their lungs. By the time James helped the woman to safety, he looked back and saw that their coach was fully consumed by flames. He knew he could not go back in, regardless of who else might have been alive inside. Within a few minutes it was over.

Maybe it was the shock of what had happened, or maybe pure exhaustion, but as James and the woman looked at each other, each said nothing for several minutes. With their chests rising and falling almost in unison, they lay down on their backs and stared upwards.

As if someone was pulling a curtain across a window, the sky was slowly covered by large plumes of dark gray smoke, which blotted out the daylight. All that could be heard was the burning of wood and the cracking of metal and glass.

Chapter VI

Captain Ben Forsythe woke to find a middle-aged black woman leaning over him, gently patting his forehead with a cloth that was dampened with cool water. It was a soothing feeling. A feeling he had rarely experienced in his life. Remembering where he was, but still groggy from the blow he'd taken to the head, he closed his eyes and drifted back into thoughts of an earlier time.

He recalled how his grandmother, who lived with his family when he was growing up, would rub his shoulders after a hard day's work on the family farm. He would relax in the main room after washing up and sit down on the bench facing the front windows where the sun was soon to be setting.

Grandma Sara would sit next to him. As he leaned forward with his arms crossed in front, she would rub his back with her withered fingers. She didn't need to have the strength of a younger woman when she knew the right places to rub.

He would look up and smile at her and sometimes give her a kiss on her cheek. Grandma Sara had always taken a special liking to Benjamin. She always called him Ben, though, reserving the full name for his mother, who used it when she felt Ben needed to double his efforts on any particular task which, unfortunately for Ben, was quite often. Ben's mother, Caroline, was a stern woman. She was originally from Boston,

Massachusetts. She had met Ben's father, David, after he had moved east to take a job. After their short engagement, they were married in a small church. A year later, Caroline gave birth to Ben.

It was in the third year of their marriage when Ben's father, David, decided to move the family back to Pennsylvania to the family farm after his own father had passed away. The farm was more than David's mother, Sara, could manage on her own, and it was a far better place in his opinion to raise a child. David had a good amount of knowledge on how to run the farm from time spent with his parents as a youth. But it was clearly more of David's dream than Caroline's, as she rarely shared the same joy he felt upon pulling in a successful crop of soybeans or earning a fair market price for their corn.

Sometimes Ben wondered what exactly his father saw in his mother, as it often seemed there was no true connection between them. When there was a disagreement between them in their home, Ben always seemed to silently side with his father, and Grandma Sara wasn't shy about standing up for Ben if she felt the child was being treated unfairly by Caroline.

Growing up on a small farm near the Susquehanna River in the heart of Susquehanna Valley, Ben had all the things a young boy could wish for. Good fishing and hunting with woods and fields to play in, a starry sky to gaze up at in the evening, a friend at a nearby farm to play with, and a Grandma with a warm spot in her heart for an inquisitive ten-year-old. Even though he was born in Boston, it was as if Ben never really knew any place farther away than the few towns closest to the farm.

When he was sixteen years of age, Grandma Sara passed away. There had been nothing in his life up to that point that showed him what true sorrow was, until now. He remembered running through the fields of corn to find a place where he felt solitude; a place far from his mother's beckoning call. He wept until his eyes swelled, until he felt he had no more tears to shed.

Life on the farm wasn't the same after Grandma Sara's passing. The bridge of peace his grandmother built, had slowly eroded and there was no one remaining who truly understood his feelings. His father wasn't the type of man to sit and listen to an adolescent's problems in life, and was often busy running the farm and trying to pay off his debt to the bank. His mother's cold, stern demeanor left him wanting so much more.

A year and a half later, Ben made the decision to join the U. S. Army. The army offered Ben a chance to focus on his future, and even though a part of Ben wanted to stay with his father and work the farm, the army offered him the chance to start anew. Now, twenty years later, his path had narrowed. Removed from his mind were the thoughts of going back to life on a farm, of marriage or ever having children of his own.

He winced from the pain and woke again.

The woman tore two narrow strips of cloth from her dress. The first she folded into the size of a half dollar. She then placed it on the wound on Captain Forsythe's arm and bound it firmly with the second strip of cloth. She did the same with the gash on his head as well. He tried to stand, but was still very dizzy. "Sara," he whispered as he plopped back down to a seated position, trying to focus on her face.

"Yes, my name is Sarah... Sarah May Atkinson. Not sure how you know it sir, but you've taken quite a blow to the head and you'd best rest for a spell."

"Glad to meet you madam, I am... I am Captain Ben Forsythe," he whispered back.

Sarah May pointed at James, who was looking over the train wreckage. "That man saved my life. Pulled me out of the burning passenger car. I haven't seen any other survivors besides us."

"Well, just so you know madam, your savior is my prisoner."

At that moment, Captain Forsythe remembered the handcuffs and looked over at James, who was no longer wearing them. He carefully checked his coat pocket and found the keys missing.

Sarah May was quick to steady his swaying and gently supported his head as she leaned the captain back onto the ground. Minutes later, as he regained his senses, he checked his side for his firearm, which he confirmed was still lashed down in its holster. Looking out upon the wreckage for his prisoner, he found James still walking amongst the burnt train cars. The captain motioned with his hands in a sweeping manner as if to shoo the woman away. "You may go about your business madam. I thank you for your kind attention, but I'll be just fine."

"Hmmf," Sarah May huffed quietly under her breath. "Just fine my foot. You've got a gash in your head and I pulled a good size piece of glass from your left arm. It appears to have bled clean and didn't seem to hit any major arteries. But you'll need rest. You're a far piece from a shiny penny."

Sarah May gathered up the remaining strips of cloth she had torn from her dress hem and tucked them in her side pocket. She placed the less-than-half-empty canteen of water she had found against Captain Forsythe's leg. "I'll be back in a while to change that bandage, and I don't take no for an answer."

Captain Forsythe said nothing in return, as no doubt it would only draw more conversation from Sarah May. He smirked slightly, admiring her sand.

Deciding to search the wreckage area before the sun set, James systematically had been walking around each burning car, looking for any items that might have been thrown free of the crash that could help their party. Starting close to the cars, he created larger circles with each lap to cover as much ground as possible. A rawhide-covered canteen of water was the first blessing, ironically lying in the middle of the dry riverbed. He shook it up and down and heard the precious liquid sloshing around inside. Opening the cap, he confirmed the container was half full.

He next found a woman's wool coat, which lay next to a boulder in the riverbed. In one of the pockets he found a woman's compact. He placed the compact in his shirt pocket and then tied the sleeves of the coat around his waist. He thought the coat would make an appropriate gift for Sarah May. The night would be cold and it might raise the woman's spirits to receive a gift that offered comfort and warmth.

Walking around the third car, he came across two dead Mexicans, their bodies lying not far from an open strongbox. He could only assume that they were part of a group of bandits who attacked the train. Inspecting their bodies, he discovered they were shot in the chest, but there were also many bruises and abrasions he couldn't account for.

The box they lay next to, appeared to have been removed from the car prior to it being torched, and the contents were clearly gone. It was too big and heavy to be of any use to them, but beside the box was a small army canvas satchel with a leather strap. It contained a mess kit consisting of a bowl, fork and knife, along with a leather-wrapped spyglass. There was also a small bag of beef jerky. James pulled the spyglass to its full length and checked the lens. It had a small crack on one edge, but seemed to work just fine.

Throwing the satchel over his shoulder, he continued his search.
He began to find hoof prints around some of the area, but they looked to have been unshod. It stood out to him as peculiar, as he had never known of Mexicans riding unshod horses before.

Twenty yards away from the last car, lay a model 1903 Springfield rifle. The caliber read .30-06 cartridge on the barrel. James removed the Mauser-style strip clip and found five cartridges inside. Working the bolt action, he found the chamber was empty. The wooden stock looked to have survived the crash without splitting, and only featured a few scrapes with a small chip on the heel of the butt end. The folding ladder sight was still straight and appeared to be adjustable for windage and elevation.

James started to have a good idea of what must have been in the strong box. The army must have planned a pick up of gold from the mine they had stopped at, and provided the best armed groups they could, to guard it. The modern army rifle was a great improvement over the older single shot Springfield model. While five rounds were not enough to fight off a group of Mexican bandits should they return, it was a vast improvement over his .32-20 revolver as well as the Captain's .45 Colt revolver.

As the sun started to set, James approached Captain Forsythe.
"I think we should keep clear of the burning wreckage tonight. We can make camp just up over that hill. Those poor souls can't be helped now, and their condition is going to bring in coyotes and other curious lot. "

"You'll get no rebuttal from me. We'll head up over the rise and make camp, but remember, Private, you're still under my custody."

James, the Captain and Sarah May spread a blanket beneath a small stand of Ponderosa pine. The moon was only a sliver in the sky, but the flames from the still burning cars cast an eerie glow, down across the dry gulch, illuminating the tall pines.

Sarah May tended to James' shoulder wound, and then changed Captain Forsythe's bandages during the night, replacing the charcoal poultice she had set under the dressing on his arm, which had borne a good size laceration. His head wound was looking free of infection, but she changed that bandage as well. None of the three survivors slept much, as they would sometimes catch a glimpse of an animal in the shadows. Most likely a coyote looking for an easy meal amongst the wreckage. James also wondered if the Mexicans would return, looking for survivors. He wondered why they didn't carry off their dead. Usually bandits left nothing behind they could use or sell, and it was strange how the Springfield rifle was left behind. He thought more about the unshod hoof prints, too.

It would be dawn in a few hours and the small group would need to decide whether to stay put with limited resources and wait for help to arrive, or move out of the dry riverbed to get a better view of their surroundings, or even yet, try and make it to the nearest town. James closed his eyes and weighed the options before falling asleep.

Chapter VII

The old Sioux brave known as Mato rode to the top of the ridge to look down on the train wreck. He was the largest and strongest of the band he rode with and, as such, was respected by some of the younger braves. Even though he was never destined to become a chief, he had fought many battles against the white man who had invaded their homeland and broken so many treaties. He remembered his people were often outnumbered and overmatched in weaponry.

He looked down at the worn 1873 Winchester in his rawhide scabbard. Dozens of scratches and dents marred the old wooden stock. Most of the bluing was worn from the barrel and receiver. It was still serviceable, but was no longer accurate past a hundred yards.

"A white man's modern army rifle would be quite the prize to bring back to my fellow braves," he thought to himself. His wardrobe was a mixed lot. His pants were made of tanned buckskin, which stopped just past his ankles. The moccasins on his feet were old and worn from many years of hard use. He wore a thin gray wool shirt with a collar, the type often seen in a dry goods store. Over the shirt he wore an old buffalo skin vest, with a few beads and charms hanging from the fringes on each side of his chest. They swung gently from side to side as he rode on. He wore no hat. His hair, which had grown well past his broad shoulders was mostly gray, and was tied behind his head with a thin leather strap, forming a tail, almost rivaling that of the dapple gray mare he rode.

He continued down the steep bank, toward the cars, which were still smoldering even though the flames were now long gone. A hazy, grey smoke, which had settled around the riverbed, swirled and parted as the brave's horse slowly walked closer to the burnt cars. The air was thick with death, but that did not deter him from his thought of bringing home a prize.

The pines surrounding the area reminded him of his youth. He remembered the tall pines and the water which flowed through the river rocks, bearing fish for his spear. But that was many years ago. Most of the great pines had been harvested for the train trestles, while others were sent back east on the long iron snake for board lumber. The past several years had brought hot, dry summers, forcing the tribes further north or west to find water to camp by. Some went to government reservations. But he chose to stay with his brother Ogaleesha and the younger braves.

Looking into a few windows of the cars, he found the entire contents consumed. He didn't agree with Ogaleesha's decision to burn the cars, or to leave behind the new soldier's rifle, but he had not survived this many summers by challenging his brother's orders. Riding around the cars, he spotted a few footprints, which piqued his curiosity. He soon learned the intention of them, as they wound around the cars in a similar manner as his own horse. For several minutes, he stopped and listened for signs of life. He removed the lash from his rifle scabbard and tugged on the stock just enough to make sure it was loose enough to be retrieved quickly if needed. Slowly following the tracks in the dirt, the brave followed them up the ridge toward a small stand of pines.

He could hear voices ahead and after a few minutes, concluded it was a conversation of two. Ducking under a few low pine branches, he stuck close to the small pines, using them for cover as he rode closer. When he stopped a second time, the talking had ceased. He dismounted his horse, quietly pulled his rifle from its scabbard and proceeded on foot. His moccasins made no sound as he circled behind where he thought the voices were coming from.

He had always been gifted with good eye sight, and even in his older years he could clearly see a woman kneeling next to a man who had his back against a tree. As the brave flanked the couple, he could see that the man wore an ivory-handled Colt revolver. Immediately, the brave raised his rifle as his face tightened and his eyes squinted with anger.

"You!" shouted the brave in Sioux tongue as he raised his rifle.

Before Captain Forsythe or Sarah May could react, a bolt was heard closing shut on a chamber from behind the old brave. He dared not fire.

"You are stealthy," the old brave said aloud as he kept facing forward, and changed his words to the English language. "But you keep poor company."

"Just leave the rifle here and go," the voice said from behind him.

The old brave lowered his Winchester and dropped it to the ground, then quickly ran off through the pines. As James watched him go, he was amazed at the how quickly the large man moved and then disappeared from view.

"You fool, why didn't you shoot him?" cried Forsythe, as he rose to his feet.

"Haven't you seen enough death these past two days? I saw him ride in alone and I didn't see why he couldn't leave that way." James didn't want to shoot anyone, especially in the back, but was already having second thoughts about letting the old brave go free, and silently wondered if it had been the wisest of ideas.

"He'll bring back others and then what will we do? You've only worsened our situation," Forsythe grumbled.

James knew Forsythe was right, but he wasn't going to admit that to him. It now made some sense as to why he had seen so many unshod hoof prints around the wreckage, and why two Mexican bodies had remained. He knew the Sioux tribes had been defeated years ago, but this southern band must have jumped their reservation. The brave he let go would most likely return with others, if they were in fact the ones who attacked the train.

"We can all walk, and we'll head out as soon as we can gather our supplies together," James said. He picked up the Sioux's Winchester and tossed it firmly to Forsythe, who caught it convincingly and cycled the lever action to check the contents of the magazine. The captain found four .44-40 shells, and quickly fed them back into the magazine.

"Which way do you propose we head, Private Riley? Do you even know where we are?"
James glared back at Captain Forsythe. "I'd sure as hell like it if you'd address me by either my first name or last name, but not as Private!"
"Fine, Mister Riley," replied Forsythe. "You're still my prisoner, but I see no reason why we can't work together given our current situation."
"Is there any particular name you'd prefer to be addressed by, madam?" Forsythe said to Sarah May with a slight lilt in his voice.
"Nope. Sarah May has always been just fine with me," she said with a smile.

"Judging by the way we came and if, that is, in fact the San Miguel Mountain range, I figure there's plenty of miles between us and the nearest town south of here," said James. "Can't say what's north of here. I expect the Sioux will ride back from the southeast. They'll figure on us to follow the train tracks out, so we should steer clear of them and stay where there's better cover. We won't be able to outpace them on foot, but if we find the right location, we could hold off an attack until help arrives. I sighted a ridge to the northwest this morning, and I think that will be our best bet for safety. They won't be able to track us as easily and they'll need to go on foot, like us. Plus, we'll get a good look at the surrounding terrain from up there."

The others agreed, and started up the path to the top of the ridge. It wasn't the best time of day to be under the hot Colorado sun, but they

didn't have a choice. They needed to put a few miles between themselves and the wreckage, should the band of Sioux return.
An hour later, they had reached the top of the ridge. Small rock outcroppings provided some cover and the surrounding brush was mostly small pines and alders, which would be more than sufficient to gather some dried branches for a fire to keep them warm after the sun went down. James found a small clearing and the group gratefully sat down for a rest.

He pulled out the canteen and passed it to Sarah May, who looked at him slightly astonished at his generosity. "Why thank you Mr. Riley. Most men wouldn't oblige me with such manners."

"It's always been 'ladies first' where I was brought up ma'am, and you can call me James."

"And you can call me Sarah May, or just Sarah if you wish. It wasn't the order in which you chose to share your canteen, James, it was the fact that most white folks would let me die of thirst before they'd let me drink from it."

James just smiled back, as nothing else needed to be said. Sarah took a few small swigs of the canteen and handed it back to James, who stood up and offered a long, outstretched arm to Captain Forsythe, who was seated a few feet away. He paused for a second, raising an eyebrow as he looked over at the woman who so kindly bandaged his wounds.
"It sure is hot in these hills," he said, as he accepted the canteen and downed a few small gulps."

He smiled at Sarah for just a fraction of a moment, but is was long enough for Sarah to notice there was something more behind his rough exterior.

James sat down next to Captain Forsythe and took a few swigs himself, sloshing the contents to get a feel for what was remaining. "The brave who rode into the gulch this morning..."

"Yes..."

"He acted like he knew you."

"I know the one called Mato," Captain Forsythe answered. "He runs with his brother who heads a renegade band of Sioux. They jumped the reservation some years back. I put a scar on his brother's ear a few years ago. If my shot had been a few inches to the left, a lot of homesteaders and miners would sleep a lot better."

"Is there a bounty on them?"

"Most likely. I was riding with the army when it happened. They wanted Mato's brother, Ogaleesha, brought back to the reservation and I was with the group that tracked them into a canyon a few years back. We were ambushed and lost several men, but not before I put a bullet through Ogaleesha's left ear. I left the army the following year and went into business as a private bounty hunter. When he reports back to his brother that he found survivors, I have little doubt they'll come looking for us."

"So how is it you came looking for me?"

"I have a long list of deserters to search for Mr. Riley, and you were just in the right place at the wrong time. Most men I bring in have started their lives over. I don't have to chase them halfway across the desert into a blind canyon to earn my pay. Most I find at a local saloon, or at some farmstead having dinner. The army pays me to bring them to justice and I serve my papers with no one getting hurt – usually."

"I don't call that much of a living," said James. "Hunting down old men who were looking for a way to start their lives over."

"Well, it's an honest living. Besides, I'm sure 'those men' were old enough to know what they were doing when they signed up for the army, weren't they?"

James didn't answer, but just stood up and walked away to the edge of the bluff and looked out onto the horizon. Captain Forsythe's sharp words soaked into James' conscience and stuck there. James knew he was expressly talking about him. He had always justified his action of leaving the army as a protest to the atrocities he had seen committed by the army. Had he been wrong to flee and move back east?

As the sun started to go down, James sat down beside the fire, and started to whittle a piece of Spanish cane he had taken from the riverbed.

"How can you just sit doing nothing, when our pursuers could soon catch up with us?" snapped Forsythe.

"I'm not just sitting; I'm whittling a flute for my new grandson. Keeping my hands busy helps clear my mind to think."

"And just what are you thinking Mr. Riley?"

"I'm thinking it's best for us to stay put for the evening. It's going to be cold tonight, and they're sure to be overconfident in their overtaking us since they have horses and we do not. My guess is they'll wait until first light before they come any further."

"Well I certainly hope your guess is right, sir."

"My daddy used to whittle," Sarah said with a smile. "He'd make pipes for his tobacco out of old roots. I can close my eyes and still see him sitting beside the creek where we lived in Tennessee. Whittling and letting the wood chips fall into the water. I used to pretend the chips were small boats floating on down the river in a race. I'd pick one out and see if it could shoot the rapids between the stones and make it to the finish line."

"Were you traveling to see your family?"

"No, my family is all gone now. My momma and my brother got sick and died not long after the war ended, and my daddy passed away last spring."

"I'm sorry to hear that," replied James.

"I, as well, ma'am," said Forsythe.

"It's alright. I'm using this opportunity to start over again. I'm on my way to San Francisco, where I'm going to open a small restaurant. Nothin' fancy, just a place where travelers can stop and get a good bite to eat. My momma taught me to cook for the family when I was only seven years old. If I'm lucky, I'll be able to see the Pacific Ocean from my new home. I've always wanted to live near the ocean. At least close enough to hear the waves crashing on the shore. I hear the Pacific is just beautiful, and bigger than anything you can imagine."

"Sounds like a very good plan," said James.

"Yessir, it is," answered Sarah. "The good Lord didn't have you pull me from that wreck, just so I can quit. No sir. I'm going to make it to San Francisco."

"I like your spirit, ma'am," added Forsythe. "I was fortunate enough to see the Pacific myself a few years back. I was on the trail of two brothers who had robbed a train in Los Angeles. They were headed for Mexico, when I caught up with them in the little town of El Cahon. They had stopped to water their horses and themselves at the same time."

"What happened?" asked Sarah.

"Let's just say that they weren't too keen on returning the money they stole."

"Oh, I see," said Sarah, softly. "Well, I'm going to look around the bend for a place with a little privacy."

"I hope my story didn't offend you. You really should sleep up here next to the fire."

"I wasn't offended Mr. Forsythe. Sometimes a lady just needs a little privacy, if you know what I mean."

"Oh, yes, of course. Please, take this." said Forsythe, as he stood up and withdrew his ivory-handled Colt from his holster. "Umm... Just in case."

"Mr Forsythe, do you really think I'm going to get attacked by a bear while I relieve myself?"

"Bear, no. But there are cougars up in these hills."

"Tell you what, I'll just break me off a switch on my way down the trail; but thank you just the same for your concern."

Forsythe watched Sarah wrap the wool coat around her shoulders and walk a ways down the trail until she rounded a corner and was out of view.

"Nice lady," said James.

"Yes, indeed. A very nice lady."

"Exactly how long have you been bounty hunting?"
"I started out as a Pinkerton agent after the Indian Wars died down. Worked about ten years guarding trains and recovering stolen money. After that I decided to go freelance, and have been ever since."

"Pays well?"

"More than enough if your good at it."

"Good with a gun, you mean?"

"Mr Riley, you may find me heartless, but I assure you, I gave every man a fair chance to come in peacefully. and just in case you have any ideas, yes, I'm a fair shot."

"I can't imagine the army having a high price on an old deserter like me, who left so many years ago."

"There were quite a few men who decided to just up and leave Mr. Riley. If you must know, the Army pays the same for every deserter, unless there are additional offenses – and no, it isn't very much in your case."
"Then why go out of your way to take me away from my family? There must be bigger fish in the pond?"

"If you must know, I wasn't hunting you. I was paid to change trains in Chicago and assist with guarding the gold shipment on this train. I remembered you from a raid on a Sioux camp many years ago. You happened to lay me out with your rifle butt, if I recall correctly."
"That was you? And after all these years you remembered me?"

"When I saw you board the train the other day, I knew I had seen you before. I searched my mind and placed you at the battle of Powder River. You see, I have a gift for remembering faces and places, Mr. Riley. Some call it a photographic type memory. Let's just say, if you hadn't struck me, I probably wouldn't have remembered your face so well. After placing you at the battle, I recalled your name and remembered you as the defiant scout who had led our squad. So when we arrived in Chicago, I wired for information on you. As it turns out you were wanted for desertion."

"They were wrong to try and burn that camp, and you know it. I decided I wasn't going to lead the army into any more encampments just so they could kill women and children. Now you're going to destroy my life and for what, a few dollars?"

Forsythe said nothing. He just stared into the low, flickering flames of the camp fire.

A few minutes later Sarah returned to the camp holding a jackrabbit in her hand.

"I figure since we have that small fire goin' we may as well have a little dinner."
James smiled at Sarah. "However did you catch that?"
"I'm not totally helpless, you know. We ate rabbit quite a bit in our family. Daddy showed me how to use a throwing stick or a rock to stun them."

"Incredible," added Forsythe.

"I don't have any cooking utensils," said Sarah, "but I'm sure Captain Forsythe can make us up a spit to roast him on."

"Yes, ma'am, I certainly can."

"I told you, you can call me Sarah, Captain Forsythe. Come to speak of it, what is your first name? I know it isn't captain."

"No ma'am, it's Benjamin. But my grandmother always called me Ben."

"Well then, if you don't mind, I'll call you Ben."

"Yes, that would be fine, Sarah." Forsythe stood up and started to walk down the trail toward some brush.

"I think I'll call you Ben as well, and you can call me James. That way we're all on a first name basis."

Ben felt the slight sarcasm in James' voice, and glared at him over his shoulder as he kept walking. He was comfortable with Sarah calling him by his first name, but didn't want to extend James the same privilege. To him, James was still a deserter in custody and his job wasn't finished until he brought him to the proper authorities. Yet, he kept thinking about James' earlier words.

It didn't take long to cut and assemble the spit, and within an hour the three were enjoying Sarah's catch.

"Funny how some of the best meals you can remember come during the strangest of times," said James.

"Probably 'cause the best meals are when you're the most hungry," added Sarah.

"Sounds about right," said James as he pulled the remaining meat off a leg bone. "If you'll excuse me, I'm going to scout a ways down the trail. I'll be back shortly."

As James walked off quietly into the night under the glow of the moon, Forsythe stared at his empty hands and placed a finger in his mouth to get the last bit of fat. The meal was small, but delicious. It had gone down so quickly.

"Here," said Sarah, holding out her hand with one of the last pieces of meat from the other leg bone.

"Oh, no, I couldn't Sarah," said Ben.

"Why, sure you could. I want you to. You know the Lord says: It's better to give than receive."

"That's what I hear," he said. Ben reached out for the piece of meat and took it from Sarah. "Surely the Lord never had your rabbit."

They both laughed.

There was something other than just her name that reminded Ben of his grandmother. "That was very generous of you."

"It made me happy too, Ben. Glad you liked my cooking."

"Have you always been so generous?" he asked as he wiped his mouth from corner to corner.

"As long as I can remember. Learned it from my daddy. He was one of the most kind and generous people I've ever known. To my way of thinking, it's a sure way for me to keep his good spirit alive."

"Never thought of it like that," said Ben as he placed a few more sticks on the small fire.

"Come on now, Ben. I'm sure you had someone in your life that passed on plenty of good habits to you as well."

"Sorry if it seems a bit foreign to me after all this time. Just not much call for generosity in my line of business."

"Never too late to learn, Ben. Never too late to learn."

"I'd like to know more about your father. Water?"

"Yes, thank you."

Ben leaned over and passed the canteen to Sarah.

"I'd be happy to share a story or two," she said smiling.

Chapter VIII

1865 (39 years earlier)

Jeremiah Atkinson sat on the bank of the creek that flowed behind his small cabin. Fishing line in hand, he had hopes of catching his family's evening meal. He had built the cabin ten years ago, right before his wife, Ellie, told him she was pregnant with their first child, Sarah.

Jeremiah had cut the trees and made them into notched logs. The roof was made from cedar shingles he had hewn from a few red cedar trees that were common to the local area. In fact, everything they had around the homestead was made by Jeremiah. He liked creating with his hands and putting in the work for his own home, rather than hiring someone else to do it. Being able to do for himself and his family gave him a great feeling of accomplishment. Once in a while the roof would leak and Ellie would call out to him: "Jeremiah, that darn roof is wettin' my kitchen table again."

"Then just move the table over a bit," he would shout back. They would both laugh and he would then be on the task of fixing the shingles. Ellie had died of the fever when Sarah was only nine.

Jeremiah did his best to raise his daughter, and made sure she went to school most days. Sometimes she would ask to help in the fields and be excused from school, but Jeremiah refused, understanding the importance of an education.

The sun shown on his chest as he cast his line into the creek. His tattered overalls had straps, which hung down off his shoulders on each side. He liked the feeling of the warm sun on him. His pappy always told him to fish on the side with the sun in your face, so as not to cast your shadow onto the water. Brook trout could be cautious like that.

Jeremiah's back and shoulders told an ugly story. The scars always reminded Sarah of flattened cane grass that had been matted down by a deer after it had bedded down for the night, with the strands crossing every which way in a random pattern. Jeremiah rarely thought of them now. He had found religion with Ellie - and with it, had thrown aside his hatred for those who had beat him. He was a free man now and he could raise his daughter and make a life for them as he saw fit. Sarah had asked him once why he had the marks on his back. He explained how he wasn't always a free man, and that the marks were made by men who did not have enough love in their hearts.

A slight tug on his line was all Jeremiah needed to pull back quickly and set the hook. A beautiful brook trout jumped and cut the surface of the water with its tail. He pulled in the line with one hand, while the other kept the tension, as he guided it over his forefinger. He gave back some line a few times to let the fish swim and tire itself. Some men preferred to fish with a pole, but Jeremiah preferred just the line, as he always felt it gave him more of a feel for the fish on the other end. He didn't worry about the line cutting into his hand, as they were heavily callused from years of hard work. They worked in concert, as he gave out and then retrieved the line as needed, until the trout was done tugging and gave up its fight. Jeremiah gently pulled it onto the bank where he quickly dispatched it by placing his thumb inside the fish's mouth and then snapping his wrist, which broke the fish's spine. He then placed it down and covered it with cool wet grass to shade it from the sun.

Hoping to catch one more for dinner, he placed another worm on his hook and with a few spinning motions, gently tossed the line back out into the creek, letting the current lead it past the large round stones where trout often lie to ambush their prey. Just then, he heard a voice behind him.

"Daddy, I'm back from schoolin'," Sarah shouted as she skipped down to the creek.

"Not so loud, child," Jeremiah replied in a baritone whisper. "You might scare the trout." Sarah placed her tablet and reader on the bank and sat down next to him. She rested her head against his shoulder and stared into the clear water, watching to see if she could spot a fish.

"Already caught one," he said. "How was school today?"

"Good," she replied. "In the morning, we each had to solve arithmetic problems. But we studied geography in the afternoon. That's my favorite. Where does the river go, Daddy?"

"I suppose it goes into a larger river, and then eventually into the ocean."

"Have you ever seen the ocean?"

"No, I haven't, but from what I understand it's bigger than anything we can imagine."

He wished he could have told her that he did, but his life's journey started and ended with Tennessee.

"Bigger than the state of Kentucky?"

"Much, much bigger, from what I've been told. Why do you ask child?"

"I was just thinking. If I was a fish, I'd swim into that larger river, and keep going until I reached the ocean, so I could see how big it was for myself."

Just then, Jeremiah's line tightened and Sarah shouted, "You got one, Daddy! Pull it in!"

"That is my intent, Sarah May."

Jeremiah landed the fish and dispatched it quickly. Placing it next to the other fish he had caught earlier, he could see the difference in size. It was much larger. Especially large for a brook trout.

"Looks like a good dinner to me, child," he said, as he smiled down at Sarah.

"I'll get the wood stove ready for cookin' and I'll make you some coffee the way you like it, Daddy," said Sarah, running back to the house ahead of Jeremiah.

Jeremiah watched her run and remembered himself at such a young age. Life was simple, and simple things were sometimes the experiences you remembered most. A hot meal and the company of his daughter. He wished he could provide her with more, but he remembered that to Sarah, the catching of the fish, the preparation of the meal and making his coffee was surely a simple and happy life.

Children don't necessarily need more to be happy. But, still, Jeremiah hoped for a good crop of tobacco this year. The tobacco was a reminder of his slavery-ridden past, but it was a cash crop he knew all too well, and he needed it to pay off. Last year's crop was meager due to poor growing conditions, but this year's crop had promise.

He had already cut the plants and hung them to dry in his barn. Soon, he could take the dried leaves to town and sell them for a good profit. He could then buy Sarah some new shoes, which she desperately needed, as she had grown at least two inches in height this year. Surely her feet had grown too. He kept a list of what he needed for the fall. Everything from shotgun shell makings to sugar, flour, and, of course, those new shoes.

He had traded one of their goats earlier in the year to a neighbor in order to get the tobacco seedlings he needed for this year's crop. The rain had been light and frequent this spring, with sunshine every other day. Now, the summer sun had come and it wasn't shy like it was in the spring. He walked to the old barn, which looked to lean to one side slightly. He placed his catch on a small wooden table just outside the entrance. A pin oak stump made a fine chair as he seated himself and started to clean the two fish with his pocket knife.

When he was done, he called to Sarah who came running and took the fish inside to pan fry them. She would place some fresh herbs and goat butter inside the fish and then add a little bit of bacon grease to the pan, just the way Jeremiah liked them to be cooked. Sarah had learned from her mother, who had been a very good cook herself.

Walking into the barn, Jeremiah checked on his drying tobacco. The entire place smelled of a slightly sweet fragrance. He pulled a few leaves down from the drying rack, crushed them in his hand and smelled them. His hands were so worn and callused from years of hard work, he had to hold the crushed mixture to his cheek to feel for any residual moisture.

"Another week," he thought to himself. He put the remaining few minutes before dinner to good use by chopping some kindling to have stove fuel for the next few days. He could smell the fish cooking from the open window in the kitchen, not too far from his chopping block.

Sarah set the table in a modest way, but always liked adding a few special touches. The plates were enameled tin and so were their cups. The napkins were well-worn and had formerly belonged to an old T-shirt or apron. But in the center of the table Sarah set a small clay vase, which held a few daisies. These had been her mother's favorite flower. The table was set for two, but a third chair remained vacant. The vase of flowers was set in front of it.

Sarah liked to make sure they were always fresh. She usually picked them on the way home from school, as it gave her a fond memory of her mother. Sarah finished her fish and wiped the goat's milk from the corner of her mouth. She poured her daddy another cup of coffee and sat back in her chair and looked out the kitchen window, watching the sun's rays get slightly lower in the sky. All that was left for Sarah to do was finish her studies before Jeremiah tucked her in bed for the night.

"Tell me about the ocean, Daddy," she said sleepily. "Tell me how it looks."

"Well, I hear it's so big that you can't see the other side."

"Like Mr. Sanderson's corn field? One time I climbed a tree and couldn't see the other side, as it went up and over a hill."

"Even bigger than that," said Jeremiah. "I hear it's as big as the whole sky and deeper than the tallest tree. Why I hear there are whales as big as a barn in it, too."

"Can we go to the ocean some day, Daddy?"

"Maybe, child. Maybe when you're older and when I don't have to grow tobacco anymore. Maybe we'll go together and catch us a huge fish."

"We'll need to get a bigger frying pan, Daddy."

Jeremiah gave her a kiss on the forehead. Then they said their prayers together and off to sleep they went. One dreaming of an ocean so blue and so vast, that was filled with all kinds of fish. The other dreamt of a promising crop, a new pair of shoes and a smile on a little girl's face.

It was Saturday of the following week, when Jeremiah pulled down all the tobacco from the barn racks in the rafters. He gently layered the dried bundles of leaves in large burlap bags and tied each one shut with a piece of jute. He loaded ten bags in all into the back of his buckboard, to which he hitched a single mule. He asked Sarah to join him on the trip into town. If he could get a fair market price, he would be paid enough to purchase everything on his list, and then some. Best of all, Sarah would have that new pair of shoes.

When they reached the town, Jeremiah drove his buckboard in front of a long barn. It was a tall structure, two stories high with an office and a small porch on the front left side. Jeremiah asked Sarah to wait in the wagon for him while he saw the man inside about his tobacco.

Sarah could smell the aged plants through the burlap bags. She fiddled with the hole in the right leg of her denim overalls. She liked her overalls a great deal, mostly because of all the pockets. They were much more fun than a dress, and Jeremiah always allowed Sarah to wear them on the weekends. She had been meaning to sew a patch onto the hole where her knee had pushed through, but she had to buy more thread first.

Within a few minutes, Jeremiah emerged from the front office with a smile of pride on his face. Sarah watched as he unloaded the bags from the buckboard and stacked them neatly on the porch. A tall thin man wearing a frock coat and a pair of thin wire frame glasses came out of the office and counted the bags and then asked Jeremiah to sign the receipt. Jeremiah did not know how to read or write, but he made his mark, which was good enough for him.

Jeremiah shook the man's hand and then climbed back into the buckboard. He smiled at Sarah and gave her a hug.

"How about we get you a pair of new shoes, child?" he asked, and then watched Sarah's eyes widen.

"Yes, Daddy!" she shouted. "We can stop at Henderson's. I bet my foot has grown a whole size!"

We're going to get quite a few things at Henderson's, and clear my bill with Mr. Henderson as well."

Jeremiah had been paid in cash, and the three hundred and ten dollars in his pocket would help him make the repairs needed to their home, as well as purchase more livestock and other necessities. It was worth all the hard work he had put in.

Arriving at Henderson's Mercantile, he helped Sarah down from the buckboard and took her hand as they walked inside. Mr. Henderson was having a conversation with two men. The men both looked to be on the older side of forty, and did not have the look of the local farmers that Jeremiah usually saw in Henderson's. One of the men wore a large knife in a sheath. The handle looked well-worn and reminded Jeremiah of some of the knives carried by the southern soldiers during the Civil War. The other man had a new shirt in his hand, which seemed quite appropriate, given that the one he had on looked rather tattered around the elbows and had the front pocket half torn.

Jeremiah figured they were from one of the local ranches, who would often hire out jobs to men on a seasonal basis. Some of the men would be from local farms who might have had a crop go bad, while others were saddle tramps, who would wander from town to town, looking for work and then spending the money often as soon as they could get paid on gambling and whiskey. Jeremiah figured the latter, since he knew many of the farmers in the local area. The man with the knife glanced over at Jeremiah with an unsavory look.

"Good day," said Jeremiah firmly, but not too loud.

"Hmmm," was all the man said as he looked Jeremiah up and down, then continued his conversation with Mr. Henderson. It was very obvious to Jeremiah where some men's hearts stood regarding their feelings toward him and his kind. It didn't seem to matter that the war was over. Something deep inside still made him feel as if he had to justify everything he did. He hoped that Sarah's life would be different than his, and that her education would be the key to unlock many doors.

"I'll take a few bottles of whiskey to go as well," barked the man in a sharp tone.

"I'm sorry, I don't sell whiskey in here," said Henderson. "If all you need is the shirt and the salt pork, I can take payment at the register."

"I'll be right with you, Jeremiah," Mr. Henderson said, as he noticed Sarah looking at the display of new leather lace-up shoes.

The man with the shirt paid Mr. Henderson and picked up the bag of salt pork as well and started for the door.

"I'll meet you over at the saloon," said the man with the knife. He walked over to a display of hats and tried a couple on, but kept an eye on Jeremiah while doing so.

"Would you like to try on some shoes, little lady?" Mr. Henderson asked.

"Yes, I would sir. But can you measure my feet first?"

"Absolutely. You just sit down right here and take off your shoes."

Mr. Henderson could see how worn Sarah's old shoes were. One of the laces had been retied a few times after breaking, and one sole had a hole worn clear through.

Mr. Henderson pulled out a peppermint stick from his apron pocket and handed it to Sarah. "Something to keep you busy, while I'm measuring," he said.

Sarah smiled, thanked him and wasted no time tasting the cool sweet treat. Jeremiah had always liked Mr. Henderson. He was a kind man who genuinely cared for people. All people. It showed.

"Well, you've grown a full size larger than what you are wearing young lady. Now let me see what I have in a size seven."

Mr. Henderson showed Sarah two pairs of shoes. One was brown and the other black. Both were lace up style boots, but the brown pair had an extra piece of leather across the front toes that made them look especially fine to Sarah.

"Daddy, can I get this pair?" she asked pointing to the brown shoes.

Jeremiah looked at the display, noting the price. "Certainly, child," he responded. Sarah smiled at him and then went back to work on the peppermint stick, twisting it around in her mouth while she savored it.

Mr. Henderson placed them on Sarah's feet and laced them up. "Not too tight?" he asked.

"No, just right. Thank you, Mr. Henderson."

"You're welcome, Sarah."

Then Sarah turned and hugged Jeremiah around the waist. "Thank you, Daddy."

"You're welcome, Sarah."

Jeremiah let Sarah walk around the store as he carried out his business with Mr. Henderson. "I want to pay off my bills in full."

"Grow a good crop this year, Jeremiah?"

"Did indeed, sir. Did indeed! Will be puttin' this salt to use when I slaughter my pigs this fall. Will be plenty to get us through the winter and some to sell as well."

Mr. Henderson took his ledger from under the counter and placed it on top, turning the pages until he found what he was looking for.

"Let's see, with the amount you owe plus the new shoes, it will be twenty-nine dollars and seventy-five cents."

"I'll be needing a few extra things as well, sir." Jeremiah handed Mr. Henderson a piece of paper, which had been folded in his pocket.

"I had Sarah do the writing," he added.

Jeremiah was slightly ashamed of not having learned how to read and write himself, but that feeling was replaced with the pride he felt for his daughter's schooling.

"I think I can fill all of this today, Jeremiah," Mr. Henderson said as he tallied everything up with a pencil. "The total will now be forty-two dollars and seven... well, we'll just call it forty-two dollars even."

The conversation was not lost on the man in the corner looking at hats. He left the store and the small bell could be heard as he closed the door behind him.

When Jeremiah left the store with Sarah, the man and his friend were nowhere to be seen. He helped Sarah into the wagon as she was still very focused on her peppermint stick. Jeremiah felt proud as they headed home with enough provisions for the weeks ahead. Sarah periodically looked down at her shoes, and then would look at Jeremiah, smiling.

As they rode on toward home, Jeremiah noticed two horses on the trail a ways behind them. They kept their distance as they rode. Jeremiah believed them to be the same two men in the store. He couldn't be sure as they were a ways back, but he didn't want to keep turning around to look. As they turned off onto another part of the road, the two men also turned off. They were now within a couple miles of their home and Jeremiah didn't want them to follow him there. As he and Sarah came up to a small pond on the right, Jeremiah decided to pull the buckboard over and stop, hoping the men would pass. Then he would know for sure who they were and what direction they were headed.

As Jeremiah looked over his shoulder, he could clearly see it was indeed the two men from town. The had come to a halt and just seemed to be watching his buckboard from a distance.

Jeremiah whispered to Sarah. "Sarah May, you listen good to Daddy. You know where we are, don't you?"

"Yes, Daddy. Our home is around the corner and over the next hill."

"That's right, child. If there is any trouble with these men, I want you to run into the house and hide there. You understand?"

"But Daddy, why should there be trouble?"

"I don't know child, I'm hoping there isn't. Just do as I say."

"Yes, Daddy."

Jeremiah never carried a gun for defense. The only gun he owned was an old shotgun that he used for game birds and he never went to town with it.

Uncomfortable with waiting for the men to make their next move, Jeremiah snapped the reins and the mule started into a fast trot. As Jeremiah drove the buckboard up the crest of the hill, he turned slightly over his shoulder to see the men behind him keeping up pace. Coming down the hill, he rounded the corner and could see his house just a quarter-mile away. Anxiously wanting to reach the security of their home, he gave another snap of the reins. Approaching the barn, Jeremiah, drove the buckboard inside and did not bother to unhitch the mule. He told Sarah to run inside the house, which she did. Jeremiah, closed the barn doors behind him and quickly followed Sarah into the house.

He felt nervous, having to rush around on his own property. He did not know for sure if the two men were following him, but it seemed as if they were down on their luck, and he was pretty sure they were drinking, since they had mentioned heading to the saloon when they were in the store.

He pulled his double barrel hammer gun down from above the door and loaded it with bird shot. He sat in a chair by the kitchen table, looking out the window and waiting to see if the men would approach. Sarah asked if she could fish for their dinner, but Jeremiah told her to wait. He had her start a fire in their stove and told her to boil some water for tea.

The two men rode up, just as Jeremiah had feared. He hadn't studied them that clearly before. It was mostly the knife, which had held his attention in the store. Now he could look them over better as they sat before him on their horses. The man with the knife wore a short-brimmed hat with a leather band. His chaps were well worn and his boots had spurs. The other man sat taller in the saddle and had on the new shirt he had purchased in town. His hat looked mashed down on his head and the brim was warped and encircled his head like a series of hills and valleys. Neither man wore a gun belt, but the taller man carried a rifle scabbard on his horse. Jeremiah couldn't make out the type, but catching a glimpse of the powder horn around the tall man's saddle, he figured it to be a black powder musket.

Jeremiah opened the window just enough to talk to the men.

"What do you want here?" Jeremiah shouted.

The man with the large knife on his belt spoke first.

"We saw you in the store earlier today mister, and thought maybe you could use some help around your farm."

Jeremiah was quick with his answer. "I can't afford to hire out. Thank you all the same."

"Well, would you be able to spare a chicken or two?" the man asked. He could see some of the birds outside of the henhouse scouring the ground for bugs.

Jeremiah had raised Sarah in a Christian manner and had always taught her to help others, but these men were not in need of help. In his mind, men who had money to gamble and spend on whiskey, didn't need a chicken. Jeremiah cut to the chase.

"You men had money to spend today. You don't need one of my chickens. I'm asking you to leave my farm, now!" He slid the double barrel along the open window sill, with only a few inches protruding. The man with the knife whispered something to the other man and the two slowly turned their horses and rode around the side of the barn and were soon out of sight.

"Can I go out and pump some water for the tea, Daddy?"

"No child, not yet. I'll let you know when you can go outside."

Jeremiah watched to see if he could catch sight of the men getting back on the road, but they didn't emerge. He was reluctant to head outside, but he reminded himself it was his property. He broke his back working this land and he wasn't going to let a couple of no-good saddle tramps steal from him. He told Sarah to close the door behind him and to bar the door until he returned.

"Daddy, I don't want you to leave me here," she said anxiously.

"I'll be back in a few minutes, child. Do as I say."

As Jeremiah stepped off his porch, he heard a shot, which was followed instantly by a loud squeal.

He remembered his pigs… They shot one of his pigs! He ran around to the back side of the barn and saw the man with the knife standing over one of his two pigs. The other man was outside the pen, holding the smoking rifle. The cloud of smoke from the black powder still hung in the air and he wasn't sure if the two men had seen him yet. He raised his shotgun at the men through the cloudy mist, but hesitated. He knew that if he pulled the trigger, he'd hang for shooting a white man. He leaned the shotgun against the barn and then charged the two men. The man with the knife stood above the hog with the long toothpick blade ready to butcher it. Before Jeremiah could close the distance, the man suddenly looked up and called out his friend with the rifle, "Emmit!"

Emmit looked up in time to see Jeremiah charging, but had no time to reload. Instead, he swung the long rifle as a club. Jeremiah tucked his head low as he lunged and planted it firmly in Emmit's stomach, just as the rifle swung above him. Emmit flew backwards, dropping the rifle and landing on his back. He tried to regain his feet, but Jeremiah was right there as he rose, swinging his fist into Emmit's face and dropping him for a second time. Emmit felt like he'd been hit by a sledge hammer.

His ears rang and he felt dizzy. The man with the knife had climbed out of the pen and came at Jeremiah with the long toothpick blade. It appeared he was no stranger to a knife fight, as he kept his stance low as he advanced. Crouching forward, he jabbed the knife at Jeremiah with quick sharp thrusts, cutting Jeremiah's left forearm. He let out a low laugh, as if happy with his handiwork and daring Jeremiah to rush in the same way he had with Emmit. Jeremiah couldn't take his eyes off the man with the knife, but he was able to circle slowly around and now could see that Emmit was still on the ground.

The man jabbed the knife at him again. This time Jeremiah jumped back out of the way of the blade, with it just barely missing his face. The third time the man came in low and tried to stab Jeremiah in the gut. Jeremiah quickly grasped the man's wrist. The man was surprised by Jeremiah's speed. He clawed at Jeremiah's face with his free hand, trying to gouge his eyes, but Jeremiah grabbed that wrist too. He squeezed with all his strength and the man cried out, dropping the knife from his hand.

Just then, Jeremiah felt a sharp pain across the back of his head. He released the man's wrists and dropped to his knees. Emmit had managed to stand and deliver a smashing blow with his rifle stock.

As Jeremiah tried to get up, he could see the man in front of him looking to regain his knife. Just then an exploding "boom" filled the air. The stock of the rifle, which Emmit had wielded as a club, splintered into a thousand fragments. Emmit screamed, grasping his face in his hands, as some of the wood had penetrated his skin, making him look like he was the victim of an angry porcupine.

The other man turned to see Sarah, in a seated position on the ground holding the smoking double barrel shotgun. The recoil had knocked her on her backside. She stood quickly and cocked the second barrel, pointing it directly at him. "Leave my daddy alone!" she cried out.

Jeremiah rose to his feet and stepped firmly on the knife with his boot and glared heavily at the man.

"You heard my daughter. Get the hell off my land!"

The two men slowly got back on their horses and rode off without saying another word. Jeremiah looked over at Sarah. Tears that were held back earlier, started to flow down her face. She dropped the shotgun and ran to her daddy.

"I'm sorry, Daddy. I'm sorry," she cried.

"You have nothin' to be sorry about chi..." he almost said 'child', but stopped himself.

He held her close to him and kissed the top of her head. "Let's go inside, Sarah. I'll make us some tea."

"What about our pig?" she asked.

"Well, I had told Mr. Henderson we were going to slaughter the pigs in the next few weeks. I guess we're just going to treat ourselves to bacon and cornbread for dinner."

Jeremiah retrieved the man's knife and made a few long cuts on the pig and left it to bleed out. He sighed as he was too familiar with the long chore that awaited him. Later that evening he went down to the stream and filled a bucket from it. He used some of the cool water to soak a rag and then placed it on Sarah's sore shoulder, which was starting to turn purple from the shotgun recoil. The remainder he put on the stove to boil and made them each a cup of tea. "Sugar in your's, Sarah?" he asked.

"Yes please, Daddy," she replied politely. As they both sat at the kitchen table sipping their tea, Sarah looked under the table, still admiring her new shoes.

"My daddy never thought of me as a child after that day," said Sarah.

"Thank you for sharing that with me. It sounds like your father wanted only the best for you," said Ben.

"He did, and I miss him very much. With my mother being gone, it was like he was living the life of a mother and father all in one. I had him buried down by our fishing spot near the creek. It is amazing the impact a good father can have on a child's upbringing. Kind of like your grandma, I imagine."

"Yes, she did have a large impact on my upbringing."
"James has his son and grandson in Montana," said Sarah. "I figure he still has some teaching to do in his life, wouldn't you say? I mean, with the gift of a new grandson and all that goes with it."

"Yes... I guess I really didn't think of that."
Ben sighed quietly as he took a sip of water from the canteen. He looked up as a few raindrops hit the brim of his hat. Soon a steady drizzle began to fall, followed by a crack of thunder that could be heard echoing across the sky. The rain picked up in tempo and soon became a downpour. Ben grabbed another blanket and sheltered Sarah's head with it.

"Well, we needed the water, and the good Lord hath provided," she said. She then lay down next to the camp fire, which was starting to go out, and layered herself with the coat James had found for her. Ben reached over and covered Sarah's head with his hat. She smiled out at him from under the brim.
"You are a kind man, Ben Forsythe," she said. "Do remember that."
Ben nodded quietly in confirmation.

Strangely, behind the smoky smell of the extinguished fire, Sarah could detect a slight hint of the former owner's perfume, embedded in the coat. It was foreign to the surroundings of the wilderness.
She closed her eyes and tried to dream of San Francisco, pretending the thunder in the distance was the crashing of ocean waves.

Chapter IX

"Look at you!" yelled Ogaleesha. "You're half the warrior you once were."

Standing a good foot shorter than his larger, but younger brother, Ogaleesha slowly circled Mato, with his gaze fixed firmly on his brother's face. The rain beat down on their teepee and thunder echoed loudly. Not to be outdone, Ogaleesha made his voice louder than the thunder.

"It wasn't long ago that you wouldn't have come back here without the white man's hair in your hand and your lance in his heart. Where is the fierce warrior that fought to avenge our people? You look tired and soft. Maybe you should go back to the reservation and sit with the elder women and tell stories to the children. Do you even remember why you were named Mato? I think the fierce bear has lost his teeth."

Mato glared back at Ogaleesha. His thoughts no longer held the admiration of a younger brother, but were rather bound by remorse.

"It is you, brother, that have weakened. Your namesake drives you with a burning obsession. I, too, hate the white man. But I fight for honor and only when necessary, I kill. It was necessary for the soldiers and it also was for the Mexicans, but the travelers on the iron horse were no threat to us, yet you burned them. Your hatred of the white people is so strong, that you would lower yourself akin to the worst of their kind, instead of looking for a way to rise above them."

"There is no strength and honor in them. They all deserve to die!" Ogaleesha snapped back.

"You are wrong. I sensed strength in the one that tracked me. He could have shot me in the back or stolen my horse if he had chosen to. We parted ways with honor."

"They are weak and their greed will be their undoing!" shouted Ogaleesha.

"You talk of greed, yet you steal from them the very gold that corrupted them. Your hatred will be your undoing," replied Mato.

"Tell me exactly what you saw," demanded Ogaleesha.

"There was the one with the ivory gun that shot you. I'm sure it was him, only he was no longer in uniform. There was a woman, too, dark in skin like the Apache. Maybe even darker. The other man was older, but silent in his approach. He moved like a Sioux. They had one canteen and a couple of rifles and maybe a revolver between them. I saw or heard no one else."

Ogaleesha nodded and stopped circling Mato.

"As long as I, Ogaleesha, lead our people, my decisions will be obeyed. We will track them and finish what we started."

The next morning brought more rain, and as dawn came the band of eight Sioux rode out to the area of the train wreck. They looked down upon the twisted metal and burnt cars. Ogaleesha did not wish to stay long, realizing that news of the delayed train would soon bring the army back to the area.

Buzzards had already started to land cautiously in the nearby trees. There had to be at least a dozen on the branches, shaking their bodies and flexing their wings every so often to shed the rain they were not used to encountering. Ogaleesha knew as soon as the rain stopped, the birds would resume circling the sky above the wreck, which would surely pinpoint the location to anyone looking for survivors. The army would come in with their rifles and shoot off the buzzards, only to find the Mexicans. They would be misled, just as Ogaleesha had planned.

The braves skirted around the rim of the ravine and rode down the far west slope until they came to the spot where Mato had spotted Forsythe. He swung his leg over his horse in front of its neck, and in one smooth motion hopped off onto the ground. He knelt beside the tracks in the dirt, which were barely visible due to the rain. He confirmed the count to Ogaleesha, who was still scowling from the fact that his brother had not killed the only witnesses to the Sioux's presence in the area.

"Yâmni," Mato said, which meant "three" in Sioux. He pointed toward the north. "No horses. They travel on foot."

Ogaleesha instructed one of the braves to stay behind and clear any sign of hoof or footprints heading north, before rejoining them.

Mato swung back up onto his saddle blanket and led the others to what was a small dirt path. It wasn't long before the trail started to become rocky and much smoother.

"The man who is light of foot leads them well," said Mato. "They go where they can see for a distance and the trail becomes narrow. We can still follow, but they will be harder to track in this rain."

"He will lead them to their death," Ogaleesha responded. He tugged at his left ear. "The one with the ivory-handled gun is with them, and I want his scalp!"

The evening was almost upon them by the time the brave who had cleared their hoof prints from the trail, caught up with Ogaleesha and the rest of their band. Mato, who was crouched near the trail looked back towards his brother. "I think they have turned off here and have gone up into the rocks, brother."

Ogaleesha laughed. "Haa, they mean to have us follow them on foot to slow the use of our horses. This man who you say is light of foot seems to have experience in the mountains. That is no matter. You will take Kohana and Otaktay and ride up into the rocks as far as you can. When you can ride no more, you will go forward on foot. They must only be a few miles ahead of us. I will take the other braves and ride around the long trail to the west toward the river. They must come out at some point, and I will be waiting for them. If they turn back, you three must capture them and bind them tight with rawhide, but save the one with the ivory gun for me. Tonight, we make camp here. Tomorrow, we finish the survivors."

Chapter X

Sarah woke as the sun started to come up. Her body was stiff from the cold ground, but the wool blanket, coat and hat had shielded her from the majority of the rain and, surprisingly, kept her mostly dry. She stretched her arms above her head and sat up slowly. The rain had stopped during the night and the air smelled clean. The sky was clearing as she looked around at the scenery. The rust brown rocks contrasted against the grayish blue sky.

It was a beautiful place, she told herself. Even with the three of them being lost, hungry and cold, it was still a beautiful place. She saw James drawing on a piece of paper. He was perched on a large rock, looking out over the terrain to the north, which was mostly still cast in cloud shadow.

"Good morning," she said. "I'll make us some breakfast. How does ham and eggs sound?" she joked.

"At least we had that delicious rabbit last night, and our canteen is now filled with water," replied James.

"Writing a letter home?" she asked.

"Actually, I'm making a map. Trying to draw where we've been and what I'm seeing up ahead. The land can paint a good picture if you know what to look for."

"Look promising?"

James looked through the spyglass. "No sign of a town yet, but I'm seeing some pretty green vegetation about five or six miles to the northwest, beyond the next rise. My guess is there is a river flowing down from the north. With the help of the rain, it should be running through that area. With any luck, we can follow the river upstream to a town. But if Ben is right and we're still being pursued, we'll need to leave soon."

"Where is Ben?" asked Sarah May.

"He said he went to stretch his legs. His turn to need a little privacy, if you know what I mean. He should be back shortly."

James studied the piece of paper a bit more, then folded it and placed it back in his shirt pocket. He then removed the cane flute from his back pants pocket. He used the tip of his pocket knife, slowly turning it to form holes in the surface of the cane.

"That will make a nice instrument for your grandson," said Sarah May.

James placed the flute in his mouth and tried to play a few notes. The resulting noise was more than a bit raspy and Sarah May giggled, as the sound tickled her funny bone. She quickly placed her hand over her mouth to silence her laughter in order to not seem rude.

"Hmm, not so nice, yet; sounds way too harsh," admitted James. "Obviously needs a bit more work. I've never made one of these before, but, as they say, there's a first time for everything."

Ben walked up the path back to their camp and stared into the wet coals from the fire, kicking them around a bit with his boots. "Did you come to a conclusion on direction?" he asked James.

"North for a bit to skirt that bluff, and then west," answered James. "It looks like a strong possibility for a river there. If so, we should be able to follow it to a town. James pulled the small pouch from his jacket pocket and dumped the remainder of the beef jerky into his hand and offered a piece to Sarah. "We'll divide what is remaining and try to make the five miles before noon."

The hot sun made the miles hard. Sarah couldn't remember a time when her feet ached so much. She kept thinking about the new shoes she wore when she was young and how her daddy worked hard for the money to get them. She put the pain out of her mind and walked on.

James kept watching the ground as they got closer to the river. The rocky terrain looked to turn to grass up ahead and he knew they would soon leave much more sign in the grasslands close to the river, than they would up here, if the Sioux were following their tracks.

"I think we should stop for a bit," he said. He got no argument from Ben, and Sarah promptly sat down on a nearby rock and removed her shoes and rubbed her stockinged feet.

James motioned to Ben with a nod of his head to speak with him away from Sarah. The two walked a bit together. "Trail's gonna change as soon as we hit that grass," said James. "Best thing would be for you to head on with Sarah. I believe I can lay a false trail and mislead our pursuers. Just keep heading west until you reach the river. Make camp upon sunset and use the blanket; make no fire. I'll meet up with you the following morning."

"That's an awful risk on your part," said Ben.

"Afraid I'll skip town, sheriff?"

Ben looked hard and honestly at James. "Not in the least," he replied. He then pulled the pair of handcuffs from his jacket pocket. "I've been thinking, I really don't have any use for these out here. Just dead weight." He tossed them into the thick scrub brush, where they would be hidden from view.

"Thank you," said James. He then took the compact from his pocket. "I'm hoping to not be far behind you. I'm going to signal with this mirror in the direction of the river tomorrow morning about an hour after sunrise. It will mean I'm following. If you don't see the signal, don't wait for me. Head to the river and follow it down."

Ben then offered James his hand and they shook.

"Keep the Springfield," said James. "It's got five rounds. I'll hang on to the Winchester. Got my .32-20, too."

"Good luck," whispered Ben under his breath, as he watched James hike up and over the hill. Ben walked back to Sarah, who was smiling at Ben.

"You did the right thing," she said.

"I hope so. He'll try and mislead the Sioux with a false trail. He asked us to head on to the river. If he's successful, he'll signal and catch up with us tomorrow."

"And if he's not?"

"He'll be ok. He's doing his job as best as he knows how."

Ben and Sarah walked until the sun was low on the horizon. Ben was confident they were close to the river, but thought it best not to go on in the dark. The ground was now full of grass and Ben used the blanket to mat down a place to sleep for the night. He covered Sarah with her coat and lay down next to her. In the morning, they would look back for James' signal.

"I can remember sitting on the front porch of our home in Pennsylvania," said Ben. "We'd watch the small bugs hover just above the tall grass before the sun went down. The trees, which were lit by the sun's last rays, were a bright green, contrasted against the darker foliage in shadow. I often wondered if those bugs only lived for one day. But

Grandma Sara said they were dancing before they settled in the grass for an evening's rest."

"I wish I could have met your grandma. Sounds like an amazing woman."

"Very much so. Two peas in a pod, as she would say. We always saw things the same way, and in many ways, she was more of a mother to me than my real mother. She looked after me, and me her. Sometimes I think I never should have left the farm after Grandma Sara passed. I should have stayed and worked the land. But that would have meant coming to terms with my real mother. Hell of a stern woman. Just wasn't very happy with her life, I guess. It was hard to watch her wear my father down to nothing."

"Where did you go after leaving the farm?"

"I joined the army with a good friend of mine who lived nearby. We had gone to school together. His name was Carl Hershaw. A curious man, Carl. Always found some way to poke fun at something, as if he just didn't take life all that serious. Neither one of us gave higher education any thought at the time; we were young and thought joining the army would be adventurous. My father didn't want me to leave and my mother really showed no preference. When we went into town to sign up, we learned they were looking for men to join the Army of the Potomac. We both ended up in the 50th Regiment, 9th Corps. The training was fun at first. We both would laugh at how strict the sergeants tried to be; but we were in good shape, two strong boys who were used to a good day's labor. Growing up hunting, we were both excellent shots with a rifle as well. We drilled over and over until we could drill in our sleep.

We would talk at night after we'd had our evening meal. Starting a cattle ranch somewhere out west was always the evening topic around the camp fire. Maybe in Montana. Nothing too big. Just hoping our army pay would be enough to get a hundred head or so after we served our time. Of course, it didn't turn out like we planned...

1862 (42 years earlier)

Carl Hershaw looked through the brass spyglass as he lay on his belly. The young doe was eating in a meadow filled with grass and ferns, surrounded by maples, oaks and birches. Ben lay by his side looking down the barrel of his Enfield rifle. The two had been part of a reconnaissance patrol for the last two weeks, and although they were not supposed to give away any hint of their position, they had seen no one during their time out and a chance to hunt was a relief from the usual camp chores and drilling.

Their patrol consisted of twelve men and at three miles out, they'd report back every other day and refill their haversacks with the same hard tack, salt and dried apples. Camp food usually depended on how skilled the cooks were, and most often the men who were assigned the chore were not used to cooking. Beans, salted pork or a piece of meat with a few pieces of potatoes was the norm, and breakfast was often the same. Coffee was boiled in an open kettle, so it was warm, but hardly something anyone would recall as coffee.

As the doe put its head back down, Carl whispered in Ben's ear. "Wait 'til she shows you her flank."

Ben barely moved. He just slowly nodded his head in agreement and flipped up the rear site on the Enfield. Seventy-five yards out, he estimated. He could taste the venison sure enough from memory. Smoked over a fire, the meat would fill their haversacks and last for weeks. It would be a welcome change from the salted meats they had been eating.

As the doe continued to feed on the meadow grass, it turned slightly and lowered its head again until it was hidden by ferns. A shot rang out from the Enfield and the doe jumped high, then ran off with the long ferns giving way to her strides as if blown by the wind. Further into the trees she ran until out of sight.

"I'm sure I got her," said Ben. "I'm sure of it."

Carl collapsed his spyglass and quickly shoved it back in its leather case. "Looked like a good hit to me through the glass. She couldn't have gone far."

Carl was up on his feet quickly and ran to where the doe had been hit. His eyes followed the ferns and grass, which were marked by her blood. Ben ran up to Carl. "See! Blood on both sides of the grass trail. The ball went clean through!"

Carl ran ahead, anxious to get to the kill. Ben walked behind at a slower pace. He had been taught to track slowly. Sometimes an animal would double back or be lying hidden under a log or hidden in tall grass. He now separated the deer's tracks from Carl's. Carl was about fifty yards ahead of Ben when he shouted, "Come on Ben, she's down," waving his hands in the air in triumph, knowing they would be the heroes of their camp.

It was then Ben saw Carl, arms still in the air, suddenly bend backwards like the shape of a bow. Something small and gold shot forth from the front of Carl's uniform. Then the report from a rifle was heard. Ben stood still for a moment, not entirely believing what had just happened. He ran to Carl as fast as he could and knelt beside him. Carl lay beside the dead doe, bleeding from his chest. Ben looked around frantically, trying to see where the shot had come from. He heard voices from the woods growing closer. He quickly stuffed his pocket handkerchief under Carl's coat, noticing the center button was clearly missing.

With his rifle and canteen slung over one shoulder, Ben lifted Carl over the other and hastily retreated from the meadow. He heard bullets whizzing by as he ran as fast as his legs could carry them. Carl weighed over 160 pounds and Ben wasn't sure how far he'd be able to run. He wasn't even sure how many men pursued them. Could it be a small scouting party, or a whole company?

Ben could see the other men from his patrol running toward him. Bullets, which whizzed past his head, had struck one of them. In a few moments, the patrol had passed Ben, as he continued to run in the opposite direction with Carl on his shoulder. Suddenly, the air erupted with rifle shots as the patrol returned fire. He looked over his shoulder briefly and saw mostly smoke from the skirmish. Men were screaming and still Ben kept running. He ran until the sounds grew fainter, and still he pressed on.

Ben estimated he had run about a mile when he stopped to rest. His upbringing on the farm had made him strong and fit, but the woods were filled with rocks and roots, which made it hard to cover ground with Carl on his back. Lowering Carl down carefully, Ben looked around. He could no longer hear the skirmish.

Was he too far from it, or was it over? Cautiously, he checked Carl's wound. He had been shot through the lower chest and the blood that stained his shirt was dark in color. Carl looked half-conscious as he moaned and asked Ben to leave him.

"Nonsense," said Ben. "You're going to be fine. We'll make it back to camp."

Ben took off his haversack and looked hastily for his roll of cotton field bandages. He was able to sit Carl up and began to tightly wrap his torso. The blood instantly colored the cloth, but Ben kept wrapping. After firmly tying off the end, he gave Carl a sip of water from his canteen. Carl looked pale and his voice softened, once again asking Ban to leave him.

Ben made sure his Enfield was loaded and thought to affix his bayonet, but decided against it, as a stand against any surviving rebels would mean he'd have to leave Carl. Lifting Carl again across his back, he continued walking through the woods toward where he thought the company would be. The path they had taken back to camp so many times before, started to become a blur as he panicked. If he was off by just a small margin, he could miss the camp. He rested once again, and this time pulled the brass compass from his pocket and checked it. He knew if he continued southwest, he'd eventually cross the small path that would lead to the camp. Exhausted, but carrying on, Ben finally found the path. It gave him a burst of adrenaline as he continued on through the woods. He was pretty sure he was less than a mile out.

Ben's arms and legs burned and the sweat that poured down from his brow stung his eyes. Catching himself several times as he started to stumble, he knew he could carry Carl no further. Placing him down, he propped Carl up against a birch tree. Mumbling incoherently, Carl couldn't drink from the canteen Ben held to his lips, and the water simply ran from his mouth.

"I'll be back Carl; I promise," said Ben. Then he ran off down the path. Within minutes he was in the camp, yelling for assistance. A handful of men followed him with a gurney down the path and back to Carl. He was lying on his side when they found him. Rolling him onto the gurney, they rushed him back to the camp.

Ben waited outside the surgeon's tent for over an hour. He had no appetite for the salted meat and beans the other men were eating. He had also avoided reporting to the captain, but he knew he'd have to do it at some point. It was foolish for him to have let off the shot that killed the deer. It had given away their position and he knew it.

The surgeon finally emerged from the tent and broke the news to Ben that Carl could not have been saved. The bullet had perforated his liver and he had lost too much blood.

Ben looked down at his bloody hands and wept. His best friend was gone. Carl had made things bearable in many ways and now that was lost. There would be no cattle ranch. The very thought of it made him physically sick. He bent over and coughed up something resembling coffee and hard tack.

Wiping his eyes with his sleeves, Ben stood up, pulled the bottom of his coat taut, and walked to the captain's tent.

He removed his cap, saluted and commenced to tell him about the meadow and how Carl was shot, and how the others in the patrol ran to confront the rebels in the woods. The whole time he spoke, he could see Carl's face in his mind. He choked once, but composed himself and finished the report.

He never mentioned the deer. Buried in his mind, cross and all, that's where it would stay. Guilt could be like that.

With night falling, another patrol was not sent out until the following day. Ben was asked to lead the men back to the meadow. Following the sounds of the crows, the patrol found nine other men dead. One was missing. The area was full of sign, which spoke to some of the rebels' losses as well, but their bodies must had been retrieved. Ben's face stared up at the sun, which sent rays streaming down through the trees. It truly was a beautiful meadow, but he felt no warmth.

Chapter XI

The rugged terrain from where James Riley lay prone was made up of a series of bluffs, each higher than the next. He had purposely laid a trail leading toward him, where he looked down on the flat below with his spyglass. He knew if the Sioux were still pursuing, they would soon come over the rise. It would be his job to delay them. If he saw nothing by midday, he'd head back to where he believed the river to be.

He had done much glassing in the army, and he knew patience was the key. Just when you thought it was time to pack up, you needed to sit and glass for thirty minutes more. It was an old hunting rule he had been taught as a youngster, and one he now found quite valuable for scouting.

The sun continued to rise in the sky, and had dried his clothing from the previous night. Sweat had started to form on his brow, and he remembered he had given Ben and Sarah the canteen. He put down the spyglass and pulled the wooden flute from his pocket and played a few notes. The tone was nice now. It would make a great present for Lewis. Again, he looked at the sun. He decided he had put in his time here and it was safe to move on. Maybe the Sioux decided to turn back after all.

James tucked the flute in his back pocket, and picked up the spyglass to close it. But it slipped from his hands and tumbled over the bluff a few feet, lodging itself between two rocks below him. He leaned over the bluff to retrieve it, but it was just out of his grasp. Before inching his body forward, he checked the horizon and spotted something moving in the distance. It looked like several riders on horseback, but he wasn't sure. He needed the spyglass. As he stretched further, the edge of the bluff crumbled and gave way, and James slid and rolled down the rocky slope for several yards, slamming his shoulder into some rocks. As he sat up, he noticed a pain coming from his shoulder. "Please don't be broken," he thought to himself.

James' attempt to regain the spyglass was clumsy, if not foolish, for he had now exposed himself to the riders in the distance. Looking around for the spyglass in haste, he chastised himself for his carelessness. Surely, several years back he wouldn't have fallen. Hell, he wouldn't have even been that foolish to have dropped it in the first place. Giving up on finding it, he started to slowly climb hand-over-hand back up to the bluff where he had left the rifle. Upon reaching the crest, he noticed his arm was now getting stiff. Maybe several years ago it wouldn't have been an issue, but his age was catching up with him and he knew it. In the past, he had ignored that feeling of aging, simply blotting it from his mind.

"Maybe this is a good way to go out," he thought to himself. He wasn't afraid of dying, but wanted time to do it properly. To leave something for Andrew and his grandson, Lewis. He thought about the flute and then wondered who would find his .32-20 Colt out here in the middle of nowhere? Would he make a good meal for the coyotes and ants? He levered a round into the Winchester and assumed the prone position once again. His older eyes did their best against the iron sights of the battle-worn rifle. What he wouldn't give for one of those modern scopes. He watched and waited. Maybe the riders hadn't seen him. He double-checked the terrain around him. "Always best to have a fallback plan," he thought to himself. He noticed a trail, which led even further up into the rocks. Childhood memories flashed in his mind of the hiding games he'd played in his youth. Switching to a second spot was risky. "Could be seen... best to stay put." He wished they would hurry.

He second-guessed himself again. Should he have sought higher ground? He'd have a better chance of defending himself, but the downside was the higher he went the less likely there would be another way down. If he got his back to a ledge they could wait him out if they had food and water. Suddenly, the riders in the distance appeared to stop.

"Quarter-mile out," James thought to himself. "Out of range."

One of the riders dismounted and was checking the ground for sign. James could clearly now count three. He had thought there would be more. "Hmmm. Three to one. Not great odds, but it could be worse."

For a moment, James was confident they had not seen him. Why check the ground if he had given away his position? But then one of the riders suddenly circled off to the north, then cut back toward his position from another angle. They could clearly see the series of bluffs ahead and were going to flank the position.

"Savvy move," he thought, as the nagging in his head got the better of him. "This spot will be exposed to the flanking rider." Staying on his belly, he backed away from the edge of the bluff until he reached the rocky formation behind him. Looking up at the tall hill, he decided, "That's my spot."

It looked steep with lots of boulders, but at least there was a small, single-track trail heading up. As he started up the trail, a bullet ricocheted off a rock near him, which was immediately followed by the report from the distant rifle. They had surely seen him and were closing fast. He dove close to the boulders for cover. Aiming at the riders, he fired the Winchester two times at the approaching men. He was nervous, unsteady, and missed both shots.

They kicked their horses and closed faster upon his position. This time, James let out part of his breath, held it and fired twice more. The horse of the flanking rider dropped from under him in a tumble of dust. The rider hit the ground hard, but surprisingly regained his feet a moment later. One of the other braves rode to him to share his mount. The running brave swung a leg up and over and up onto the back of the pony.

James worked the lever again and the empty shell ejected, making a ringing sound as it bounced off a nearby rock. The rifle was empty. Discarding it, he hurried up the trail until it came to an end. Nothing above him now, but the cliff wall with rocks and brush. He knew he needed to go higher still. They would be here in less than a minute. He checked his Colt. Five rounds of .32-20. That was all.

James could now clearly see the three Sioux warriors roughly a hundred feet below him at the base of the trail. He watched from behind the rocks and brush, as the Sioux surveyed the steep grade leading up to the top of the bluff. He could see them speaking to each other, but they were too far away for him to hear what they were saying.

He needed to slow them down. Make them think twice.

Taking his time to aim his revolver carefully, he fired his Colt twice into the group, and the brave closest to him fell backwards with a yelp. The other two fired up at James blindly, but he quickly ducked behind a rock and the bullets ricocheted off into the sky.

James looked above him and saw something he hadn't noticed before. It was another small ledge about thirty feet up that looked to be no more than twenty feet wide. That was where he needed to be. There was no way anyone could flank him from that perch. Somehow, James needed to get himself to that upper crest on the bluff.

He looked down on the single track trail again and could now see the two braves slowly coming up. As he climbed further into the rocks, he felt the burning pain in his arm growing worse. He hesitated for a moment, but continued to fight through the pain. There were a few small scrub bushes along the ledge wall, which occasionally provided something to grab onto as he climbed.

It was well past midday, and the thought of Ben and Sarah reaching the river gave him a small burst of adrenaline. It had been his plan to cause these Sioux to come for him and not them! He felt his anger rising... but there was no way he was going down without a fight. The last of the small scrub grew out of the side of the bluff four feet above him. He spotted a section of root protruding from the steep incline in the shape of a cup handle. He used it to get a good handhold and dug the tips of his cowboy boots into the dirt as he pulled himself up a few feet more.

He gently switched hands on the root so he could reach up with his good arm, hoping to find the right rock that would hold his weight. Blindly groping above his head, he found what felt like a good handhold, but when he pulled down on it, it gave way, along with a small handful of dirt and pebbles that showered down upon his head. Again, he dug his toes firmly into the soil and reached above him. This time he found a rock that held firm. He pulled himself up enough to get his left boot into the section of root. He tilted his head slowly upward. Another ten feet and he'd be there.

His arm ached from the burning pain and he tried to push it out of his head. Again, he reached up and ran his hand left to right above his head until he found the right handhold. He gave one last great effort and dug his aged fingers into the dirt and clawed his way to the edge of the cliff face. Swinging one leg up, he was able to catch the edge of his right spur in the dirt. He reached up with his good arm and pulled himself up and over onto the small ledge. After catching his breath, he sat up and looked around at the area on which he sat. He had been right in his assessment, as the small patch of ground was roughly twenty feet long and only ten feet wide.

He stood up and walked over to the cliff face and rested his back against it. It was an eagle's perch if there ever was one. There was no brush on the ledge, and anyone climbing up after him could be seen coming from either side. There was no way he was going to fool the two with his effort to climb here. Once they looked up and saw the small ledge, it would be quite obvious where he was. But this was not a tactic to fool his pursuers, but rather to say, "Here I sit. If you want me, you're going to have to climb up and get me."

James wondered how they would come for him. Would they climb up at the same time, one from the left and one from the right, or would they simply wait him out? He had no water and with three rounds remaining in his .32-20 revolver, he could hardly afford to take the offensive. Or could he?

He looked around for rocks he could use as weapons, but could only find two on his perch, and they were slightly smaller than his fist. He gathered them up and placed them by his side as he tried to think of a strategy. If he simply waited, he'd most likely have to fight two opponents coming at him from different directions. But if he lay on his belly on the edge of the ledge, he could try to pick off at least one of the Sioux and improve his odds. They couldn't come at him from behind. This much he knew. They would soon be on the landing below him. If he was to attack, he needed to do it soon.

The decision was made. He moved over to the edge to look out and lie in wait. The Sioux were very good at what they do. Years of hunting and fighting had sharpened their predatory skills. He listened for them, but could not hear them. A few minutes went by, and then James caught sight of one of the warriors below. He crawled up behind a small bush and signaled something to his partner, who was out of James' view. Moving past the bush, the brave exposed himself. He looked around at first not knowing where James had gone. But then he saw the debris James had knocked loose. By the time the Sioux warrior looked up in his direction, it was too late. James fired his revolver at the warrior, catching him in the chest. The Sioux shouted out in pain and lifted his rifle toward James. A second shot came from the revolver and struck the Sioux warrior in the head. His body shuddered and bent as he fell backwards. James could hear him rolling down the slope through the brush until his body came to rest against a large boulder.

James quickly scanned for the second Sioux, but couldn't see his position. A shot rang out and a clump of dirt shot up from the ground in front of James, nearly hitting him in the face. James looked down to the left and saw the Sioux warrior advancing with his rifle in his hands. Firing his revolver again, he grazed the warrior in his side.

He had fired his last round. He backed away from the edge of the ledge and sat with his back to the cliff wall. He clutched one of the rocks in his right hand – and waited. He needed an idea. Ripping one of the sleeves from his shirt, he tore it again into two strips and tied them end to end. He then tied a loop in one end. James could hear noise coming from below, which sounded like small rocks tumbling down the cliff face. Suddenly, his perch didn't seem so secure any more.

James placed the hand of his good arm through the loop he had made from the cloth and cinched it down on his wrist. The other end of the cloth he held in the same hand. Just then a large hand appeared over the edge and dug its fingers into the top of the ledge; another quickly followed. It was only a matter of seconds before the figure hoisted himself up onto the edge of the bluff. As the Sioux stood upright, James could see he had left his rifle behind to make the climb.

Before him stood the large Sioux warrior he remembered encountering at the train wreckage. He now had serious second thoughts over his decision to let him go. His shoulders seemed to span well over two feet and he estimated his height at six-foot-six. James had always been known for his height, but the Sioux even towered over him. The Sioux warrior slowly pulled a large knife from his sheath and took a crouched stance with arms spread wide.

James placed his first rock into the make-shift sling and began swinging it above his head. As the massive Sioux warrior took a step closer, James released his sling and the rock hurled forward with amazing speed, catching the Sioux in the side of his head. The warrior seemed stunned as he placed his large paw-of-a-hand against his head and felt blood flowing from the wound. Enraged, he yelled something in Sioux at James and advanced with great speed.

James had already placed the second rock in his sling, but barely had time to start swinging it, when the large Sioux was upon him. Instead of letting the rock fly, James could only aim the rock-laden cloth into the side of the warrior's head, which stopped him mid-charge. James then kicked as hard as he could at the warrior's arm that held the knife. He felt like he had kicked a tree, as a sharp pain shot up his shin. But the blow achieved the desired effect, as the knife shot forth from the warrior's grasp. James then swung his good arm at the Sioux and caught him squarely on the jaw with his fist. The punch, which would usually send most men reeling, merely caused the Sioux to stagger a bit.

He grabbed the cloth around James' wrist and pulled him toward him. As his large arms encompassed him, he began to bear hug James.

His strength was such that James' feet were lifted off the ground and he found himself quickly losing his breath. James swung his head forward as fast as he could and caught the massive man above his nose. He quickly repeated the maneuver and this time James could hear the bone crack as blood spurted out, causing the Sioux to loosen his grip on James. By suddenly kneeling, James slipped free of his grasp and then swung another right into the side of the large Sioux's jaw. The warrior struck back with a kick that sent James flying, with his back and head slamming into the cliff wall.

Before James could react, the warrior had one hand around his neck and with the other, scooped James up above his head and tossed him to the ground like a rag doll. James could hear a "crack" as he hit the ground and a sharp pain shot up his back. The large warrior was on top of him instantly, straddling his chest as he closed his large hands around James' neck. Struggling to breath, James tried everything he could to get his adversary off of him. He found he could not reach far enough to get at the warrior's throat and he was not strong enough to break his grip. His hands flailed as he tried to strike the warrior's face. He was panicking and he knew it. It was hard to think. He felt around him on the ground with his hands, hoping to come up with the knife, a rock, anything. But he found nothing. His vision began to cloud.

Then he remembered: "The flute!" He blindly groped for his right back pocket. Was it still even there?

He could feel it, but it was broken. That must have been the crack he heard. Split in two long sections, he grabbed one. Then in one fleeting fast motion, he swung his arm around, stabbing the large warrior through his left eye. The giant Sioux screamed in agony and instantly let James go as he clutched his face and rolled over on his back. He furiously ripped the section of reed from his bloody eye socket and tried to get to his feet. James was amazed at the man's fortitude. He just wouldn't quit.

As the Sioux warrior tried to stand, James kicked him under his chin, causing him to stagger and back up. James then jumped off the ground at the huge target, slamming both his feet into the warrior's chest, forcing him backwards off the ledge. When James gathered himself and looked over the edge, he could see the twisted form of the large warrior laying still on the ground below.

Chapter XII

Sarah and Ben followed the sound of flowing water over the hill and could now see the river only forty yards below them. They had looked back several times, but had not seen any signal from James. They decided to follow the hill down, which led to an embankment, which then dropped to an area of sand and rock along the river's edge. The water was dark and churning with the silt and sand thrown downstream by the heavy rain from the previous night.

"This isn't going to be easy," Ben thought to himself. Occasionally, he could see parts of tree limbs floating past, but they were moving by at a very fast speed. If he and Sarah were to wade in, they would risk being swept away.

"We'll make our way down to the water," he said to Sarah. "It's moving too fast to wade into the river here, but we can follow that stretch of rocky ground alongside it. The river might be calmer if it hits an open stretch further downstream."

The embankment, which was a slightly steep, twenty-foot drop to the river, was filled with loose sand and rocks. Ben asked Sarah to sit on the edge. "Take hold of the sling on my Springfield rifle," Ben said. "I'll hold the barrel and slowly lower you down toward the water's edge."

Close to the bottom, Sarah let go of the sling and slid down the remaining few feet of sand on her behind. She stood up on one of the boulders at the river's edge and started to shake off the sand from her dress.

Ben was about to follow Sarah, when a shot rang out from behind him. He ducked and heard the bullet whiz past his head, but his momentary sense of relief abruptly ended when Sarah screamed. Ben looked over in time to see her body spin around and fall backwards into the river. "Sarah!" Ben yelled.

Another bullet ricocheted off a rock near his feet, and he looked up to see the Sioux warrior he recognized as Ogaleesha on top of the hill and four braves riding down the hill toward the riverbank.

Ben's only cover was to immediately drop over the embankment and lay flat. With just a small part of his upper body exposed, Ben brought the big Springfield up to his shoulder. Like a battlefield general, Ogaleesha stayed at the top of the hill and let his braves rush in first. With a round already chambered in his rifle, Ben fired at the closest brave, striking him in the chest and knocking him from the saddle with the big 220-grain bullet. Another brave raised his rifle and yelled out a battle cry as his heels kicked his horse's flank as it charged forward. Ben worked the bolt action of the Springfield and quickly fired another round. The warrior's cry stopped short as the bullet struck the brave directly in the throat. He pitched backwards sharply and rolled off his horse, raising a plume of dust as he hit the hard ground.

The third brave fired his rifle at Ben, but missed. The bullet kicked up dust and debris close enough to Ben's face that some of the dirt got in his eyes. Ben fired his next round almost blindly, but still managed to hit the brave in the shoulder and drop him from his horse. Ben tried to work another round into the rifle, but the empty brass got jammed in the receiver. Before he could clear it, the brave was upon him. He leapt from the edge of the embankment and landed on Ben, rolling them both down toward the rocks below. After seeing Ben and the other Sioux Indian tumbling over the embankment, the fourth brave charged in with his lance in hand.

Ben lost his grip on his Springfield rifle and focused on wrestling with the brave, who now had the advantage of facing him from on top. The brave pulled a knife from a rawhide skin sheath with his good arm. Ben used his opposite hand to catch the wrist of the brave. The Sioux warrior was very strong and Ben had to use both hands to hold the knife at bay. Gambling, he released one hand and quickly slid the Colt from its sheath and fired a round point-blank into the brave's abdomen. Then another into his chest. The brave moaned something in Sioux, which Ben did not understand, and then went limp.

Just as Ben rolled the brave off of him, the other Sioux reined in his horse just shy of the embankment, preparing to throw his lance. The moment Ben caught a glimpse of the spear flying toward him with feather adornments flapping in the wind, he quickly rolled to one side.

The flint-knapped point of the lance glanced off the nearby rocks close to his chest. As Ben stood up, the brave leaped off of the embankment towards him, reminding Ben of a large desert puma that would pounce on an antelope from its perch.

Side-stepping, Ben quickly palmed the hammer of his Colt .45 four times, hoping one of the bullets would hit its mark. Two of them struck home, and the brave landed on some rocks close to Ben with a resounding thud.

Ogaleesha had ridden down the hill and was now at the edge of the embankment on his dapple grey horse, with rifle held high in hand.

Ben thumbed back the hammer and pulled the hair trigger on his Colt, only to hear a heart-breaking click. It was empty. Holstering his gun, Ben grabbed the nearby lance and rose to his feet. He crouched low, swaying back and forth to give the large Sioux warrior an unsure target. Ogaleesha brought the rifle to his shoulder and fired. The bullet struck Ben in the left side, but only grazed him. Instead of throwing the lance, Ben decided to charge up the twenty-foot embankment as fast as he could. He ran erratically, trying to keep the dapple grey's head between himself and that rifle, so as not to give the Sioux leader an easy target.

As Ogaleesha turned his horse sideways to get a better shot, Ben jammed the lance into the horse's chest just under its front right leg. The horse jumped back with a squeal and then reared up on its back legs, throwing Ogaleesha from his mount. Ben quickly tried to recover the lance from the horse's chest, but it was stuck. The horse jumped back again and pulled the lance out of Ben's hand.

Ben knew that he couldn't afford to give the Sioux warrior time to recover his gun from the sage grass. So he immediately leapt at Ogaleesha, catching him off guard as he was rising to his feet. Ben grabbed at his long hair with one hand and pulling forward, landed a hard right punch to the Sioux's face. He could see the warrior spit blood from his mouth as he quickly struck back at Ben with his own fist, catching him across the side of his head. Ben's ear rang as the Sioux pulled him forward by the shirt collar and, rolling on his back, placed his feet on Ben's chest and flipped Ben over onto his back.

Ogaleesha then turned quickly to look for his fallen rifle. Before he could locate it, Ben was on his feet charging at him. Ben placed his head straight into the Sioux's gut and the two fell over the bank, grappling while they rolled down to the rocks below. Ben was close enough to smell the warrior's breath. He could clearly see the scar on the partial ear he had given the Sioux all those years ago. Each tried to gain the upper hand over the other. Pushing away from Ben, Ogaleesha rolled to the side and pulled his knife from his sheath. Ben then pulled the Colt from his holster and began wielding it like a club.

Ogaleesha jabbed at Ben, trying to force him back toward the water, where he might lose his footing. Ben pulled the revolver back past his shoulder and let it fly as hard as he could throw. It struck Ogaleesha between his neck and shoulder. Ben could have sworn he heard the crack of a bone and the Sioux warrior winced for only a second. With hateful eyes, he leapt at Ben and the two of them fell back into the swift flowing water.

From under the water, Ben could feel Ogaleesha's knife slash along his side and run across his ribs. Air bubbles escaped from his mouth as he screamed in pain. When the two rose to the surface again, Ben could see they were floating quickly toward some large rocks that broke the surface of the water. As the river washed them closer, Ben caught

Ogaleesha's wrist as the warrior attempted to stab him again. As they came upon the rocks, Ben slammed Ogaleesha's hand into the nearest one. The knife flew into the air, then landed with a splash and was quickly lost below the surface. Ben grabbed at Ogaleesha's hair with his other hand and pulled his head close enough to where he could finally grab at the Sioux's throat. Ogaleesha frantically tried to do the same. Locked in each other's grip, they sank below the surface of the turbulent, fast-moving water.

Half a mile down the river, Sarah May Atkinson clung desperately to the surface of a large rock. She remembered hearing the shot and feeling the sharp pain in her shoulder before falling into the cold river, but had no idea how she ended up at this point. There was a great pain coming from the back of her head that was stronger than anything she had ever felt before. She wanted to feel her head to check if it was bleeding, but she dared not let go of holding the rock with both hands in the swift current. The pain in her left shoulder seared through her body, and she didn't know how much longer she could hold onto her perch.

Sarah started to feel nauseous and dizzy, and her vision became cloudy. It was if the day was turning to night. She could barely make out the shore on the right side of the river where the water seemed to be flowing more slowly. Fearing that if she blacked out, she would certainly drown, she decided to make an attempt to get to the riverbank. In pain, tired and cold, she summoned the courage to push off from the rock. She swam as hard as she could, moving diagonally to the river current and letting it ease her closer to shore, until she eventually reached the quieter waters, and then the rocky bank.

Sarah crawled onto the wet ground and could feel the river-washed pebbles beneath her fingers, but had trouble seeing them. Exhausted, she lay on her stomach with her face on the rocky sand and gave way to the darkness that overcame her.

Chapter XIII

"Sarah..." She could hear a voice calling her name. Then again. "Sarah..."

Sarah May opened her eyes but could not see who was calling her. Night must have fallen as she had drifted in and out of consciousness. She was still sleepy, but recognized it was Ben's voice. "I'm here," she called out. "I'm over here!"

She heard footsteps getting closer, moving over the rocky terrain. Her head still hurt, and as she touched the back of it, she felt a sharp pain. She must have hit it on a rock while she was swept through the current. She pulled her hand away quickly, as even touching the area was excruciating.

"Sarah!" Ben called out again. The footsteps quickened their pace as they grew closer to her, but still she could not see him. She was startled when he reached out to her and grabbed her arms. "It's okay, Sarah," he said. "Everything is going to be alright." Ben hugged her and looked at her shoulder. "I need to check this," he said, loosening the hook and eye closure near the neck of her dress and then pulling the material off her shoulder to attend to the wound.

"It looks to have gone clean through Sarah, and I don't think it broke any bones."

It was then that Sarah noticed a warm feeling on her leg. It was the sun. "Ben, how long has it been since I was separated from you?"

"Why, only a couple hours. The river washed me downstream a ways and I swam to reach the bank. Then I walked further downstream for what seemed like another hour, hoping I would find you."

"I can't see you, Ben," she said quietly. Then her voice started to panic. "I can't see you! I think I'm blind!"

Ben hugged Sarah to calm her, but she jerked away when his hand started to cradle her head. "I think my head is cut, Ben." Gently moving her damp hair, Ben could see a gash across the back of her head roughly three inches across. He tore sections of cloth strips from both shirt sleeves for makeshift bandages to wrap her shoulder and head wounds. Sarah winced from the pain, but tried to remain strong.

"We'll get out of here yet, Sarah. Don't worry, please. Try and think positive. It's possible that your blindness is only temporary."

"How am I going to get out of here, if I can't see?"

"I'll carry you if I have to. Please, lie back and try to get some rest." Ben gathered some nearby sage grass and balled it up to make a soft cushion to place under Sarah's head.

"I'm going to cross downstream where it's calmer, and then backtrack along the riverbank and see if I can find one of the Indian's horses. I'm pretty sure we were only washed about a mile or two downstream. I'm hoping the horses didn't wander too far off.

"What about James?" she asked.

"If he's alive, he'll have to find his own way out, Sarah. He knew what he was doing when he suggested we split up. I sure hope he fared well. Rest now. I'll be back soon."

Ben walked the riverbank for over a mile. He stopped to wash out the wounds on his side. The area where the bullet had grazed him sat slightly below where Ogaleesha's knife had run across his ribs. The knife cut seemed to be the more serious of the two. Looking around, he recognized the large rock up ahead where Sarah had been standing when she was shot. Nearby, lay his ivory-handled Colt revolver. He had lost his gun belt to the river, so he tucked the empty revolver in the front of his pants in a cross-draw fashion.

Scanning the bank, he quickly located the still bodies of the Sioux braves. Searching them, he found a belt pouch on one of the braves. He untied the pouch from the warrior's waist, pulled the flap back and looked inside. Wrapped in a piece of deer hide was what looked to be a crude flint, a striker and some char cloth. There was also a small bundle of what looked to be dried birch bark. He tied the pouch across his own waist and continued to look around until he found Ogaleesha's rifle in the river grass. He ejected six .44-40 cartridges from the magazine. Loading the rounds back into the magazine, he took the rifle with him.

He decided to cut several pieces of buckskin from one of the dead Sioux warrior's leggings. He could use the buckskin for bandaging the wounds he and Sarah needed to tend to, and it would be stronger than the shirt cloth he'd been using. He next found a saddle blanket that must have come off one of the horses. He threw it over his shoulder and kept walking. He figured he only had a few hours before the sun went down, so he decided to just walk another half-mile or so and then head back to Sarah. Using the blanket over his shoulder as a sort of sling, he started to gather whatever dried wood he could find along the way so he could make a fire for her. He found some pony tracks along the river, but they seemed to head further away from Sarah. Walking until the river started to bend again, he decided to turn back.

The sun had just started to go down when Ben came across the spot where he'd crossed the river earlier. Holding the firewood bundle with rifle and pouch high, he waded across again, then walked back upstream to where Sarah lie waiting.

"It's only me," he said from several yards distance, as not to startle her.

"Did you bring dinner?" she quipped.

"You amuse me, Sarah. Most people who have gone through your experience would be scared to death, and here you sit, joking about dinner. I admire your courage, woman."

"I am scared, Ben. Very scared. I just don't like to show it, that's all."

"Well, I may not have brought dinner, but we now have the means for fire."

"Sounds good to me," she replied. "Nothin' takes the sting out of the cold night air, like a good fire."

"Oh, I could think of another one, Sarah, but whiskey will have to wait for now."

Thirty minutes later, Ben was still trying to get the fire going. Having grown used to the convenience of matches was becoming very evident. Sarah listened to the click of each try as Ben came down with the iron striker against the stone shard. She was sure any minute now, she would hear his voice ring out in success. But with Ben's occasional cussing, she decided to keep quiet. She could remember from her youth, her daddy trying to thread a needle in order to darn her socks. Sweat had beaded on his brow and she had not dared speak during her father's intense concentration.

Suddenly, Ben got an idea. He ejected one of the cartridges and worked out the lead bullet with the striker. He then poured the powder onto a patch, and lay it atop the tinder bundle. He struck the striker against the stone shard, and the spark lit the power in a quick flash. Ben gently blew on the small flames until they grew in size.

"Eureka!" he shouted. As the flames consumed the tinder, he quickly added some other small pieces from what he had gathered, being careful not to smother his masterpiece. Sarah could feel the comforting heat, and she scooted closer to the fire with her hands held out in front of her to carefully judge the distance.

"Time to change that bandage," Ben said.
"I was just getting comfortable," Sarah shot back. "But ok, I guess I can let you tend to me for a change."

Ben smiled and rinsed the cloth out in the river, then held it near the flames to warm the bandage before retying it around Sarah's head.

"Can you see anything, yet?" he asked gently.

"It's hard to tell," she answered softly. "I'm not sure if I'm seeing some faint light or if my head thinks there is light because of the warmth.

"Can you see my hand?"
Ben moved his hand in front of the flames as if to have the silhouette stand out.

"No. I cannot," she replied. Then Sarah paused for a moment. "Let's just take pleasure in the warmth for now. The good Lord will get us back home soon. I can feel it."

Sarah could not see the smile of admiration on Ben's face; but it was there just the same.

The sun had just come up over the hills behind the riverbank when Ben awoke. He looked at the fire, which now only consisted of smoldering coals. The wood he had gathered was exhausted, and seeing that Sarah was still sleeping, he quietly walked away to find more for their fire. What little he found had gotten washed up on the bank and was not as dry as the wood he had found yesterday. He placed some of the grass and twigs on the fire, hoping it would ignite the larger pieces, but it did not.

"I always heard where there was smoke, there was fire," he thought to himself. "It seems all we have is smoke."

As the wind changed slightly, the smoke wafted in Sarah's direction and she woke with a few coughs.
"What's for breakfast?" she asked as she gently touched her shoulder to judge if there was swelling.

"Oh, I thought you liked dinner so much, I'd whip up the same for breakfast."

"If you can shoot me a rabbit, I'd be most grateful."

"I just might do that, Sarah. But first I'm going to check your bandages."

Ben noticed the bleeding from her shoulder wound had stopped, but her head clearly needed stitches. His own side looked raw and he was hoping infection would not set in.

He tried to keep her mind on something else. "Heck, If I'm lucky enough to bag a rabbit, we might be able to cook it in the coals."

Ben worked the .44-40 rifle lever to make sure he had a cartridge in the chamber and then walked past Sarah up the riverbank.

"Ben, I was only joking. Please stay. I'm... I'm scared."

Ben walked over to Sarah and gave her a hug, patting her softly on her back, like his grandma used to do with him when he was younger. "It's okay, I understand. We'll get walking soon and follow the river out of here. I can always try and bag some game on the way."

Several miles away, James Riley had followed any available sign he could see and finally arrived at the river's edge. Riding a Sioux pony and trailing another behind him, he had tracked the remaining Sioux warriors on horseback to this very spot. But he was now wishing he had not found them.

He levered a round into the Winchester he had picked up from his fight with the Sioux the day before. As he fired it into the air, crows and buzzards jumped off of their claims and flew a short way, only to land again in small cedars and watch. James turned over the corpses one by one. Some were killed by a single rifle bullet, while another by a revolver. He looked in the tall grass for Ben and Sarah, and breathed a sigh of relief when he did not find either of their bodies. He looked down and studied the ground as if a story was being told. It was his gift, and at the age of sixty-one it had not left him. He circled the area and read the signs as if reading a newspaper... the way the braves fell and landed, the impression where Ben Forsythe lay prone, the jammed Springfield on the ground and lastly, the small spatter of blood on a large river rock with the many boot and moccasin prints on the river's edge. The story was becoming clear, but not finished.

Chapter XIV

Ben walked with Sarah along the river's edge. The walking was tricky, with Ben having to guide Sarah along the stones and sand. But the shade was best along the river. And even though walking along the bank limited their view, the river provided them with a source of water they desperately needed.

Every mile or so, Ben would walk up the bank to look over its edge and check for some sign of civilization. When the sun was at its zenith, he and Sarah took a break in the shade of a piñon pine and drank from the cool water of the river. He'd kept an eye out for a jack rabbit or sage grouse, but so far they had come across no game. He wasn't too concerned, as he knew that as long as they had water to drink, they could go another week without food if need be. But he was almost certain they would come across someone before then. Ben gathered some firewood and happened across a long piece of cedar, which had been washed smooth from the river. It would make a fine walking stick for Sarah.

When dusk came, Ben used the flint to make another fire. It went a little smoother the second time around. He had lost his jacket to the river, so he shared the saddle blanket with Sarah, draping it over both their shoulders. "It's going to be okay," he kept telling her. Sarah leaned her head on his shoulder. "I know it is, Ben. Who knows, maybe we'll turn up on someone's farm tomorrow, looking a sight to behold. You suppose James made it out and is on his way for help?"

"I don't know Sarah. I wish I had taken the chance to thank him for trying to divert the Sioux away from us. It didn't work out exactly how he wanted, but I know he meant well. I sure hope he made it."

"I think he knew you trusted him, Ben, and that might have been what mattered to him the most."

"Maybe so, Sarah. Maybe so."

The next day, Ben and Sarah walked two more miles before resting. By midday, Sarah's ankles were quite sore from the riverbed rocks, but she didn't mention a word about her pain. The walking stick gave her a little more confidence. And she found herself listening to all of the sounds she might have taken for granted previously, like the splashing of the river on the rocks, and the birds chirping in the pines and brush. There was even the rough sound of Ben's beard stubble when he rubbed his hand over his chin. She knew when she heard that, he was about to say something, as if he were contemplating the right thought.

Ben sat Sarah down by the river's edge and guided her hands down to the water to get a drink. Sarah cupped the water in her hands and drank while Ben ran up the riverbank as he periodically did.

A few minutes later Ben called out. "Sarah! I can see something a ways off. It looks like a small shack!"

Ben ran back down to Sarah and helped guide her up the side of the riverbank. The structure looked to be about a half mile away, set amongst the sage grass and a few small pines. The area surrounding it was hilly and marked with small scrub brush and rocks. As they walked through the grass, Ben could see where at one time there might have been a path between the shack and the river.

Approaching the small shack, Ben seated Sarah in the shade at the base of a pine and asked her to wait for him while he checked out the area. Ben walked slowly toward the shack after making sure there was a round in the chamber of his Winchester. The shack looked to be roughly fifteen by twenty feet in size with a corral made from cedar poles off to one side. In the center of the corral was a five-foot-tall post, which appeared to be firmly set in the ground. The structure looked old, but in decent condition, with the roof missing a few shingles here and there. The corral, by comparison, looked more recently built.

He walked past an anvil, which lay on top of a large pine stump and was held in place by several large bent nails. A hammer lay upon it. And a worn axe leaned against the wall near the front door. Beside it was a wooden bucket. Ben called out loudly enough for anyone inside to hear, but there was no answer. Slowly and quietly lifting the iron latch, he pushed open the door with his foot, keeping the Winchester close to his body and pointing forward. Kicking the door open further, he quickly stepped inside and swung the barrel of the rifle from side to side as he surveyed the room.

A few small, surprised field mice scampered out of the light from the entryway and ran under the floor boards. Several iron traps, a few snares, an old rawhide-wrapped canteen and what looked to be some jerked beef hung from the rafters. A few mining pans were stacked on a shelf near the door. Ben tore off a small piece of the jerky and tested it. It was old, but seemed well preserved by wood smoke and tasted like venison. It would do. A table with one chair was in the center of the floor and a small cot with a few blankets lay in the back corner. There was a stone fireplace made from river rocks and an iron crane, which held a small Dutch oven. Inside the fireplace were a few burnt pieces of cedar. He touched them and felt no warmth.

A modest mantle made of pine was built onto the fireplace. On the mantle, rested a lantern and a cardboard box of ammunition. Ben picked up the box of ammo and blew the dust from the top. "Union Metallic Cartridge Company, 45 Colt's 250 grain bullets" it read. Opening the box, he found four rounds. He opened the gate of the revolver and filled the cylinder, placing the hammer down on the empty chamber.

Ben next shook the lantern close to his ear and raised an eyebrow when he heard the promising slosh of kerosene inside. At least they had shelter and a little food. It didn't appear anyone was coming back anytime soon. He then walked outside and went to Sarah, who rose to her feet. After escorting her inside, he slowly led her around the shack so she could get a feel for her surroundings. He walked her to the cot in the corner and the table and chair in the middle of the room. She tapped the table with her walking stick and then the chair. Ben helped her sit so she could rest by the table. He then took the bucket and walked back to the river to fill it with water.

When Ben returned, he poured some of the water in the dutch oven. Using the axe, he then cut a slab of the dried venison and placed it in the water to rehydrate the meat so it would be easier for them to chew. That evening, Ben unrolled a blanket in front of the fireplace and made sure to position the Winchester within arm's reach. Sarah lay back on the cot, covered by a blanket and listening to the small crackles and pops from the cedar wood Ben had placed on the fire.

"Goodnight, Ben," she said.

"Goodnight, Sarah May," he answered.

The conversation was short, and they slept well, for it was the most peace they had enjoyed in the past several days.

The following morning, Ben checked Sarah's wounds again. "I feel a tad feverish," she said softly. "Nothin' too bad, mind you... Just a tad." Ben used some of the water in the canteen to clean the wound again and re-wrap it. He noticed the area around it looked slightly swollen, but said nothing to Sarah, for fear it would just upset her further. "I'm gonna' climb the hill behind the shack this morning and try and get a bearing on our surroundings. I promise I'll get you out of here, Sarah. You just rest for a spell while I'm gone."

Ben then took a small piece of the venison along with the canteen and started his hike into the hills, hoping to see another house in the distance or maybe even a town if he was lucky. He thought about the shack as he climbed. The look of it gave him the impression it belonged to one person. Maybe a miner who at one time was panning the river. It made sense, considering the overgrown trail that led down to the river. Maybe whoever lived here left when the gold ran out and intended to come back, but never did. That might explain why some of their goods were left behind. But it didn't really explain the corral, which looked to be built to hold horses or cattle. Then he remembered the center post. He had seen one like it years ago in Texas. The post was used to rein in a wild horse, which would then be fit with a saddle and green broke. And that just didn't seem to fit with a miner's shack.

After an hour of climbing into the hills, Ben saw what looked to be a wooden sluice and a small opening in the slope of the nearby hill. As he walked closer, he could see it was a mining shaft opening. Maybe the prospectors found some ore in the area and decided it might be more profitable than panning. It would have been a long ways to haul water to the sluice.

He walked inside the low-cut shaft a few yards and smelled the musty air. The beams looked to be poorly constructed from rough cut pine, and as he leaned on one of them, some dirt and dust crumbled and fell to the ground. Looking down to shield his eyes from the falling debris, he noticed several sets of footprints on the ground. He couldn't tell if they were fresh or old, as the inside of the shaft was well protected from the elements. As he ducked his head under a low hung beam, he noticed a figure on the ground. It had two arrows protruding through the cloth from the back of a tattered shirt. He pulled one of the arrows free from the cloth and could clearly see tribal markings on its shaft.

"Poor fella," he whispered as he tossed the arrow to the ground.

Hearing a creaking sound from above, he had no interest in going any farther, as he remembered the stories he'd heard about miners getting buried under shaft cave-ins. As he turned around to study how the bright sky contrasted against the dark interior, something else caught his eye behind a pile of rocks near one of the shaft walls. As he leaned closer, he could see it was several cloth sacks bound with rawhide lacing. Dirt had been shoveled on top of them to hide their appearance.

He looked back into the shaft, listening for any sounds of a person. "Hello..." he shouted, listening for the echo to fade and waiting to hear if there was a response. No one answered. He grabbed one of the sacks and felt the heavy weight of the small bundle. Untying the lacing he looked inside. At first glance, it looked to be a bag of sand. But as he poured some into his hand, he noticed the yellow color.

"Gold!" he confirmed.

He retied the sack and placed it with the others, piling dirt back on top. Ben left the shaft and continued his hike up the hills until he reached the top. He could see what looked like a trail in the distance. It was west of the river and led away to the southwest.

"This was to be their way out," he thought to himself. The day was growing warm and he finished what remained of the water in his canteen. He would simply refill it before heading back to the cabin. Walking down to the river, he thought again about the bags of gold. He contemplated carrying them out and cashing in on the lot. The bags could be worth thousands. But he stopped himself before his thoughts grew stronger. Maybe someone would come back for them, but more importantly, there was no way he could get Sarah back safely and carry the extra weight. He really had no idea how far they would have to walk, even after reaching the trail in the distance. He pushed all thoughts of gold out of his mind.

When Ben reached the river, he knelt down and started to fill the canteen. As he stooped over, looking down at the bubbles emerging from the container, he heard a sound from downstream, like the click of one rock off another. He quickly looked up and saw a lone rider trailing a horse at a slow pace.

"Riley!" Ben shouted.

Quickly placing the stopper back in the canteen, Ben ran down to river's edge toward James. He was riding with one arm in a sling, but looked to be alright.

Then Ben noticed the horses that had belonged to the Sioux warriors. "I see you found the Sioux ponies. I had a run-in with their previous owners a couple of days back."

"They were making meal for the buzzards and crows when I came across them," James answered. "Is Sarah with you?"

"Yes, she's alive... but... she's blind."

"Blind?" James asked, shocked.

"Yes. Must have hit her head in the current something fierce. She was also shot in the shoulder by one of the braves. Luckily, the bullet passed clean through. Today she woke with the chills and I'm worried about her. We found a small shack and this morning I located a trail west of here. Should be able to make good time with the ponies."

James climbed down and motioned with his finger to Ben's side where his shirt was blood-stained. "Looks like you didn't get off scot-free."

"Look who's talking," replied Ben. He lightly poked James in the shoulder for good measure. We weren't sure if we were going to see you again. I just want you to know that it was mighty big, what you did back there. Might not have worked out perfectly, but we're all still here."

"Should have worked better."

"All the same, I appreciate it... James."

James smiled at Ben as he climbed down and watered the two horses while Ben finished filling the canteen and started to walk back up the hill.

Back at the shack, Sarah stretched and sat up on the cot. She still felt feverish and had trouble sleeping. Ben had been gone for what felt like a few hours and she was starting to worry. She wished she could see the sun. When she was young and waiting for her daddy to come home she would look at the sun as it hung low in the sky. When it touched the tree tops, she knew he would be home from work soon. She felt a wave of hopelessness come over her, thinking she might never see the sun again.

Reaching for her walking stick, she felt restless and needed to stretch her legs. The floor boards of the shack creaked under her feet as she tapped her stick from side to side in front of her, searching for the table. When her stick struck one of the legs, she remembered that the jerked venison hung above it close by. She raised one hand to search for it, while keeping the other on her stick to steady herself. She touched the steel traps and pulled her hand back. The chains made a ringing sound as they swung and clanged against each other. Her next effort found the dried meat. She pulled it down from the rafter and sat at the table, tearing off a small piece. Eating the venison took her mind off her fever for a short while, but she was still worried about Ben. She prayed he would walk through the door at any moment. Then she folded her arms and rested her head upon them.

Suddenly, there was a creaking sound from the door. She lifted her head quickly as the door swung open. She could feel the breeze from outside flow in and around her.

"Ben! I'm so glad you're back. I was worried about you. Did you find any sign of a town or road?"

There was no answer. Sarah stood up and quickly reached for her walking stick.

"Ben?"

A floor board creaked slightly. Then she heard the scuff of a foot on the wooden floor as if someone was dragging one leg as they walked. Sarah waved her stick in front of her in an effort to make contact with someone or something. She could smell someone there. It was an ugly smell. The smell of sweat and musk. She heard another creak and a dragging sound.

Sarah screamed as loud as she could. "Ben!! Ben!!"

She backed up quickly, but in her haste, she fell to the ground. She crawled quickly toward the fireplace, her hands searching for something. She found the wooden bucket. She clutched it to her chest, like a child would a doll, as if the object could bring her some comfort. She heard the ringing sound of the chains as they were pulled down from the rafters. The traps made a heavy thud as they struck the table. The chains rattled and rang against each other as she heard another step come closer to her.

She screamed again. "Please, go away! ...Bennnn!!"

Suddenly a shot rang out from the doorway. A voice in front of her made a hideous moan, something almost animal. Then two more shots rang out, followed by a loud thud that made Sarah jump. A body had hit the floor.

James ran up to the shack, where he found Ben, Winchester in hand, standing in the open doorway. Ben lay the rifle by the doorway and helped Sarah to her feet, she dropped the bucket and clung to him. She squeezed him with all her strength and the tears flowed.

Blood ran from the mouth of Ogaleesha, as he lay dead on the dusty wooden floor. His eyes, still open, seemed to be staring out the door at the quiet, empty prairie.

Chapter XV

Ben sat in the waiting room of Dr. Woodward's office in the town of Dolores. Both he and James had been attended to by Doc Woodward's nurse, but another hour had passed and Sarah was still in the treatment room. The clock on the wall ticked with a rhythm that made every minute seem like ten.

James came through the front door, breaking the silence. He sat down next to Ben.

"Sent word to my family that I'll be arriving in a few days. I can catch the train out of Durango. My family and I thank you for that."

Ben half-smiled and nodded in approval, but didn't say anything. His face looked tired, and James noticed Ben's tension by observing his hands, and how he kept folding them over each other and squeezing his fingers.

"Doc Woodward seems like a good man. I'm sure Sarah will be alright," said James.

Ben suddenly changed the subject, as if he wanted to get something off his chest.

"I'm real sorry for putting you on that train, James. Real sorry."

"We're past that now, Ben."

"I'm not past it yet. I mean, it's not just that. I'm sorry for a lot of things. I'm going to leave that line of work altogether. I'm going to start over somewhere. Maybe go back east...sell the farm and... oh, I don't know..."

James put a hand on Ben's shoulder and gave him a nudge. "Come on, let's get something to eat and look into a place to hole up for the night. Doc's probably gonna be a while with her, and she'll need all the rest she can get."

As they stood up to leave, a door opened behind them and Doctor Woodward stepped out. He asked for the two men to see him in his office.

"Do either of you gentlemen know if Ms. Atkinson has any family around here?"

"No, I mean, she doesn't. She has no cousins that we know of, and her immediate family has passed," said Ben.

"She's resting now. I've got her head and shoulder patched up as good as I can. Please understand, I'm just a small town doctor. Mostly I set broken bones and treat fevers. She's going to need better care than I can give her here. I'm going to recommend sending her to Durango. There's a doctor there named Edward Pine. He's a top-notch surgeon who studied back east. I call on him every now and then for advice. He should be able to recommend the right treatment for Ms. Atkinson. It's a half a day's ride and you're welcome to borrow my buckboard. I can get along without it, as I have a dapple grey pulling my buggy. I use the other horse for odd chores."

"Thank you," said Ben. "We much appreciate your generosity. I'll settle up for whatever we owe you when I return."

The next day, Ben, James, and Sarah rode to Durango in Doc Woodward's buckboard. Ben had pitched some hay into the back of the buckboard, and on top of that, stretched out a few blankets, so Sarah could lay down for the short journey.

After reaching Doctor Edward Pine's office, they reluctantly said goodbye to Sarah. It was difficult to leave Sarah there, but Ben knew it was the best chance for Sarah to get the proper care she needed.

Ben then drove James to the Durango train station.
"Good luck with your new family," said Ben, offering James his hand.

"And good luck with your new life," said James, shaking Ben's hand. "I hope everything works out for you."

The train pulled out of the station, with its whistle blowing white steam as the wheels gradually turned faster. James leaned his head back against the window and thought of how very fortunate he was to have his family. For the first time in many years, he felt a calm come over him, like a weight being lifted from his body. He looked out the window at the desert scenery. Maybe he would come back here some day.

The following day, Ben went to the dry goods store. He unbuckled his gun belt, wrapped it up and tucked it under his arm. Ben walked up to the case holding a few revolvers. None were as nice as his.

"Can I show you something in the case?" asked the man behind the counter.

"Are you the owner of this store?" asked Ben.

"Yes, I am. David Webb is my name. How can I help you, sir?"

"Well, I'd like to sell this revolver. It's a first model Colt Single Action Army. Ivory grips are in excellent condition."

Ben opened the gate on the cylinder and handed the revolver to David.

"Hmmm," he said, as he closed the gate and worked the action. "Seems solid. I can give you twenty dollars."

"Need to have thirty."

"Hmmm, she is pretty. I can do twenty-five."

"Hell, the grips are worth ten alone. Twenty-seven."

"Ok, Twenty-seven."

Ben placed the revolver on the glass case.

"What about the holster and belt?" asked David.

"They're three dollars," said Ben with a slight smile.

"Ok. Thirty for the whole rig."

Ben then drove the buckboard back to the town of Delores, arriving at Doc Woodward's office.
The doc opened the door after he heard the horse trot up to the front of his office.
"Didn't ya think I'd make good?" asked Ben.
"I had no doubts you'd return the buckboard," the doc answered.
"How is the woman you brought here?"

"Sarah May, she's in good hands. The doc in Durango says her sight might come back. Can't guarantee, but in the meantime, he's going to recommend a school in Arizona, so Sarah can learn to live without her sight as other folk do."

"That's fine," said Doc Woodward. "But I imagine a school like that would be mighty expensive."
"It is," said Ben. "Now, about the buckboard – I'd like to buy it."

"Buy it?"

"Yep, the horse and wagon both. How much, Doc?"

"Well, I don't exactly know. The wagon is a bit old, but the horse is sound. Not sure I really want to sell."

"You said you had another horse to pull your buggy."

"I did at that. Okay, I'll sell her and the buckboard for ninety dollars. I think that's a fair price, given that she's only eight years old and well broke."

"Can I give you thirty now and pay you the rest in a few days' time?"

"You seemed to care an awful lot for that woman you brought in, and you came back as you promised. Okay, I'll trust you. Stop by next week and we'll settle up."

Ben drove the buckboard back up into the hills. He knew the way by memory. He wondered if the shack would still be vacant. After an hour, he rounded a bend and could see it in the distance. There stood the shack with its make-shift corral.

He saw no sign of any living soul. As he rode up to the shack, he looked up past the corral, into the hills. He could see the wooden platform he and James had built, set high upon four cedar poles. Upon the platform lay the corpse of Ogaleesha. The vultures had done a pretty thorough job of picking him over, and one of his arm bones hung over the side. His leather clothing was mostly intact and his hair blew in the breeze. Ben originally wanted to leave his body covered with sand and rocks, but James knew the people of the Sioux and said it should be done right, regardless of his character. This was how the Sioux left their dead, staring up to the sky.

As Ben looked further up into the hills, he could faintly see where the mine was located. He got down from the buckboard and patted the horse on his neck. He took a leather-wrapped canteen and a long, thin strap of leather from the back of the buckboard, then walked up to the shack. Opening the door, he looked around. It appeared the same as when he was last there. When his eyes spotted the dried blood stains on the floor, he quickly stepped backwards and closed the door. He now wanted to get what he came for and leave this place forever.

The sun was hot and Ben stopped to quench his thirst as he walked higher into the hills. When he reached the opening of the mine, his spirits once again soared. He felt like a kid before Christmas morning. If the gold was still there, it would go a long way to starting over. He entered the cool dark space and called out.

"Hello! Anyone here?"
There was no answer, so he walked further inside. He saw the familiar pile of rocks by the wall of the mine and quickly moved them aside. Before him, was four cloth sacks. Each was about the size of a small one-pound bag of coffee. He opened one of the sacks and poured a small amount of the yellow sand in his hand.
"Like Sarah May once said, the good Lord hath provided," he murmured. "Hallelujah!" he shouted, with the word echoing through the mine.

He took the thin leather strap he'd carried from the buckboard and tied each end to two bags of gold, then swung them over his shoulder to evenly distribute the weight. Taking another sip from his canteen, he walked back down the hill.

Chapter XVI

Eight months later

Ben pulled back on the reins from his seat on the buckboard and set the hand brake. He sighed as he looked up at the sign in front of the small building. "Prescott School for the Blind" it read. He climbed down and stomped his boots on the boardwalk several times to knock off the modest coating of snow.

It was rare for snow in this part of Arizona, but an inch had fallen during the night. He figured it would be gone very soon. He looked over at the team of two horses hitched to his rig. "I still miss that old revolver," he whispered to himself. One of the horses snorted, as if on cue, to show his contempt for the comment. Selling his Colt was something he thought he would never do, but over the past several months, he had grown used to not having the extra few pounds on his right hip.

Ben walked up the steps of the school and knocked on the door. After a few minutes, he was greeted at the front door by a young gentleman who was neatly dressed in a starched shirt and vest. He also wore a pair of tinted glasses and held a thin cane in his left hand. He didn't put any weight on it, but held it rather lightly and tapped the end against the inside of the door frame. "May I help you?" asked the young man.

"Yes. My name is Ben Forsythe. I'm here to see Sarah May Atkinson," answered Ben. "She knows I'm coming, as I wired her a week ago."

"Come in," said the young man. "My name is Samuel."

Samuel extended his hand toward Ben.

"Nice to meet you, sir," said Ben as he removed his hat and shook Samuel's hand.

He had seen many men get injured fighting in the Civil War and Indian Wars, but he had never known or cared to see the outcome of any of them. He simply saw them carted off to an Army Hospital. Now he stood before a young man who could no longer see the world, but seemed to function with confidence and grace as he made his way back down the hallway and up a flight of stairs.

Ben sat on a small bench in the foyer. He held his hat in one hand and spun it by the brim with the other, which was a habit of his when he was nervous. He must have turned the hat for a few minutes when he heard someone coming back. Ben looked to the top of the stairs. It was Sarah. She wore a beautiful blue dress and held a slim wooden cane in one hand and used it to work her way down the stairs, with one hand on the bannister and the other working the cane back and forth in front of her. When she came to the bottom of the stairs, she could faintly see a tall form silhouetted by the light from the windows.

"Ben?" she asked.

"Yes, it's me Sarah." Ben left his hat on the bench and quickly stood up.

He walked forward and gently offered his hand to her. Realizing she couldn't see it, he continued to reach out until he touched her hand. Sarah pulled him in toward her and hugged him.

"Oh Ben, I'm so glad you are here. It's been a while and I wondered what had happened to you."

"It's good to see you again, Sarah. Like I said in my letter, I had to settle some things back east. This may sound strange, but about a month ago I started to feel like something was missing. I thought about it for a while, and decided what I was really missing was your company."

"I've missed you too, Ben. I'm so glad you wrote me and decided to come out here. I had Mrs. Tanner read me your letter several times. She speaks very highly of you. She told me you donated a lot of money to the school. That was extremely generous, Ben."

"Well, I didn't ride all the way out here to discuss me. I'd like to take you to dinner tonight, if that would be alright? We could catch up on things there."

"Why certainly. I'd love to, Ben. There is a nice inn just down the street a piece. I haven't been there, but I've heard it has pretty good food."

"It does," said Samuel, accidentally giving away his eavesdropping position from behind the stairs.

"Samuel?" asked Sarah.

"Yes, ma'am?"

"I'll be having dinner with my good friend this evening. I'll be back later tonight."

"Yes ma'am. I'll go let Mrs. Tanner know."

After Sarah readied herself, Ben escorted her out to the buckboard and helped her up. They rode to the inn, which seemed to be bustling with customers. Sarah could smell the aroma of food cooking in the kitchen from outside the door.

"Mmmm. That does smell good," said Sarah. "I'm guessing fried chicken with mashed potatoes."

"I'm not one to argue with you, Sarah May," said Ben with a slight chuckle. "I think you hit the nail on the head."

Sarah May laughed. "Remember that rabbit I cooked for us?"

"I sure do. Best I had ever eaten."

Ben offered Sarah his arm and walked in. They were given a table by the fireplace. Sarah could see small flashes of light from the flames. And she could make out the silhouette of Ben across from her.

"You were right, Ben. It's a good school. Mrs. Tanner has taught me so much. Here I was thinkin' I was an independent woman. First in my family to be declared truly free. That freedom seemed to vanish when I lost my sight. I felt like a little baby, swept away from the safety of her mama's arms. Mrs. Tanner and others at the school helped me get my independence back, Ben."

"You always did have plenty of sand, Sarah. Maybe that's what I like best about you. You had a dream and followed it out west. I'm betting this won't stop you, either."

"I don't think it will. I can see shadows here and there, but I will admit, some days are surely better than others. One day at a time they tell me. But I really do feel like I'll see again one day. It's as if I lost one blessing and gained another. I can hear and smell things that I didn't pay much mind to before. Funny, how that works."

Sarah took the napkin from the table and gently pulled it out from underneath the silverware. She folded it once and held it up to her nose.

"The soap they used to wash these had a touch of lavender."

Ben took his napkin and did likewise.

"Amazing. It does have a hint of lavender. I wouldn't have thought to check."

"Lots of things have signs on them, Ben. You just have to take the time to look, and that's not always done with your eyes. Speaking of looking for signs, what ever happened to James?"

"After we left you at the school, I drove James to the station in Durango. From there he went on to Montana to see his family."

"You did the right thing to let him go on his way," said Sarah.

"Well, that's not all. You remember how I wrote you about the gold I found back by that desert shack?"

"Yes. You had mentioned donating a good sum to the school."

"That's right, but I also had wired James a third. As I figured it could benefit his new family – seein' we went through so much together."

"You're a changed man, Mister Forsythe."

"I'm convinced of that now," replied Ben. "I feel like I've wasted so much of my life these past several years, trying to get some satisfaction from making others pay for their mistakes. But really, it felt like I was trying to suppress something inside of me that was hurt. Maybe I just needed to fix my own mistakes."

"Well, that's past you now. Given any thought to your future?"

"I gave it a lot of thought. First, I decided to leave the bounty hunter business to the army, and then I went back east to sell the farm. The house was pretty dilapidated and the fields were overgrown. At my age, it would have been too much for me to work anyhow. Sold it to a young couple just starting out."

"Where will you go now?" Sarah asked.

"Well, I purchased a small piece of land in La Jolla, California. It's a small, quaint town compared to San Francisco, but I thought a small town would be a good place to start over, away from the busy city life."

Just then, the waiter came over and took their order. Ben ordered the chicken dinner for each of them and a bottle of red wine.

"I haven't had wine in ages," said Sarah. "Thank you for thinking of that."

"Another experience for you to relive," said Ben.

"I'd never heard of La Jolla before, but it sounds peaceful."

"Well, that's one of the reasons I wanted to come see you, Sarah. I know this may seem sudden, but I want to ask if you would like to go with me. Business might be slow at first, but I heard the small town was growing and could use a sort of general store. I was hoping maybe you could help me run it. I was thinking that together, we could make it work."

Sarah smiled and reached across the table to Ben. He held out his hand and she cupped it in hers. "I think that would be a grand adventure!"

She wiped a tear from her eye as the waiter came back with their wine.

"Here we are sir, one bottle of our house red." He opened the bottle and poured a little in Ben's glass. Ben took Sarah's hand and gently passed the glass to her. She held it to her nose and described to Ben the plum and vanilla she smelled. She smiled and took a sip, then nodded in satisfaction.

"It's a good one!" said Ben to the waiter, who proceeded to fill their wine glasses and then walk back to the kitchen after placing the bottle on their table.

"Here's to two friends and a new life together," said Ben.

"Together!" said Sarah, as they sipped their wine.

The next day, Sarah made arrangements to leave the school and travel to California with Ben, promising to write once a month and let the school know how they were both getting along. Sarah joked with Ben about the potential hazards of taking the train. They laughed for a brief moment, but stopped suddenly. Ben then broke the silence with a wonderful idea.

To share the experience of the country and camping under the night sky, he would take Sarah to California in the buckboard. It was the dry season and Ben trusted they would have good weather. The wagon could carry extra water and all the supplies they would need for the two of them and the horses.

Sarah agreed to the grand idea. Once on the trail, Ben cooked Sarah meals during the day, and Sarah sang songs with him by the campfire in the evening. Some were from his grandmother and some were from her father. It was a fine five-day trip.

On the afternoon of the fifth day, Ben stopped the buckboard and set the hand brake. He helped Sarah down and held her hand as they walked together down a path which led to a small house. Sarah felt the sandy soil under her shoes and listened to the birds in the distance that sang calls of which she had never heard. She could smell the sweet fragrance of the wild roses, which grew alongside the front porch. At first, she thought she heard the wind blowing in the distance. She asked Ben to guide her toward the sound. As they walked past the house, the sound grew louder. She could tell it was not the wind at all, but the sea! She stopped and dropped to her knees. Ben knelt down next to her.

Sarah swore she could see a slight shimmer of light reflecting off a faint canvas of blue, as she heard Ben say: "We're home, Sarah... we're home."

Made in the USA
Middletown, DE
19 January 2018